Wedding Receptions That Rock!

*Creative Ideas for Music
and a Fun, High-Energy Celebration*

Rich Amooi

Edited by Patricia Fogarty

Cover design by Mariela Mihaylova

Author photograph by Lucie Silveira at luciexyz.com

Newlyweds on cover: Dave and Katie Orsburn

Cover photograph by Jeff and Julie Photography at jeffandjuliephotography.com

Table of Contents

Introduction

Congratulations on your engagement! It's a pretty exciting time in your life, I know. I got married just a few years ago. And like you, my wife, Silvi, and I wanted everything to be perfect and most important . . . *fun*!

You may already be able to picture your wedding day. If you are like most couples, you would like all the guests to dance and have an incredible time. The smiles, the laughter, the fun . . . all of that is achievable. All you need is the right DJ, the right plan, and the right attitude. I've written this book to help guide you in the right direction — toward a wedding reception that you and your guests will never forget.

As a professional wedding DJ for more than twenty-five years, I have entertained at more than 1,500 wedding receptions and earned the title "Best DJ in Silicon Valley" two years in a row from readers of the *San Jose Mercury News,* one of the most respected newspapers in the country. I am an active member of the American Disc Jockey Association and have sat on the board as vice-president of the National Association of Catering and Events. I've pretty much seen it all, and I'm confident I can help you.

Let's face it, thousands of boring wedding receptions happen every year. You may have even been to one or two or five of them (I certainly have). The blame tends to fall on the bride and groom or the DJ, or all three. In many cases, DJ's just don't have the personality and experience to lead clients in the right direction, to give them advice, or to know what to do when something unexpected happens. The sad part is, they still get paid. And their clients (and their clients' guests) are the ones who suffer the consequences. You've probably heard horror stories about nightmare DJ's or terrible wedding receptions. I want to help you to avoid having one of those.

For now, take your focus off the decorations, the wedding dress, the Chiavari chairs, the place card holders, the sashes and linens, the flowers, and the venue. Those things won't help you have a fun reception. Not one bit. While they certainly have their place, it's your guests and the activities during the reception that will create the joy and excitement timeless memories are made of.

The single greatest opportunity your guests will have to flaunt those emotions will be when they join together on the dance floor and create a synergy that can be generated only by those who are dearest to you. The entertainment is the driving force that makes people remember the maid of honor kicking off her shoes and the groomsmen pulling off their ties.

People create memories.

I've DJ'ed at some of the most exclusive country clubs, mansions, wineries, and private estates in the San Francisco Bay Area. But I also led an outrageous, memorable, and super-fun wedding reception in a humble backyard that had no landscaping and lots of noise from the busy street in front of the house. Did I mention the great view of the trash can, recycle area, and chicken coop, and the discarded tractor tires? None of that mattered, though. The newlyweds had an incredible time with their family and friends because they made the entertainment a priority. And because they planned *everything* with the guests in mind.

I know it's your wedding day. But it's not all about you.

Focus on what matters. Focus on your guests. Focus on the entertainment. Focus on the little things in between. That's what people are going to remember from your wedding day. That's what will get them pumped up and ready to dance. You want your guests to feel as if you've really thought about what *they'd* like when it comes to music, activities, entertainment, and dancing, instead of just thinking about what you like.

What types of things can you do to make your reception rock? You can do a bunch of little things that will add up to make a huge difference. And in the following chapters, I've outlined all of them for you. You should be able to read this book easily in a sitting or two and come away with some great ideas for your reception.

Wedding Receptions That Rock! is for anyone planning a wedding reception. It doesn't matter if you are going to have a laid-back, barbecue-chicken, paper-plate, corn-on-the-cob reception for 50 people in your parents' backyard or a top-shelf, tequila-shooting, tabletop-dancing, off-the-hook, $200-a-plate madhouse of a reception for 400 guests at the most prestigious country club in your area. Many of the tips I provide can apply to either scenario.

Although I do give you a few things to think about for *before* the reception, the main focus of this book will be on the events *at* your wedding reception. Specifically, you'll need to think about the entertainment, the activities you choose, the timing, the flow, and the unique things you and your DJ can do to make the party more fun and really memorable for everyone.

I will cover the schedule of events for the reception: the introductions, the meal, the music, the special dances, the cake-cutting, the bouquet and garter tosses, interactive games, and everything in between.

Obviously, you're not going to use every idea I share with you. Plenty of these tips will help you with your planning, though. Every little bit helps, right? Just take what works for you and ignore the rest! And of course, feel free to jump ahead or skip sections that may not be relevant to you.

I've also spent countless hours researching and chatting with recently married brides from across the country to come up with my "Top 25 Wedding Regrets" (see Chapter Thirteen). As I compiled this information, I was surprised to find an astonishing number of the same regrets popping up; many of these mistakes are repeated by brides and grooms over and over again. But that's because they didn't have the info you are about to receive! The list is pretty fascinating and a great lesson for anyone planning a wedding.

You'll notice that I talk about "energy" numerous times in this book. That's because the DJ's job is to *build energy*. Energy is connected to the flow at a wedding reception. One of the ways energy is built is by seamlessly moving from one unique event to another. The more energy at your reception, the more exciting it will be — and the more likely your guests will be dancing.

There are certain things and activities that build energy, and there are certain things that kill it. I will be covering both categories in this book. I've tried to make my advice as straightforward and easy as possible so you don't get overwhelmed. Speaking of which . . .

There are certain things you can do right now, at this very moment, while this book is in your hand, to get off to a fabulous start. At the top of the list is your attitude. Try to stay positive during the planning process. Remember that the main function of a wedding reception is *not* to try to impress your friends. That's where most people make their first mistake and put too much pressure on themselves.

Very simply, your wedding reception is a celebration, a party. The top two things the guests will most likely remember are the food and the fun. Since I am nowhere near an expert on food, I will skip that part and just help you with the fun.

My wish for you is that you have an absolutely incredible wedding celebration, one you will remember for the rest of your life.

Okay, let's get to work!

Chapter One

Before the Big Day

Before I jump into helping you with the actual reception, let's consider a few things that could have an impact on your celebration before you and your guests even get there. You may not think that these considerations have anything to do with the DJ or the fun, but they do. All are connected to the energy we are trying to build. If one thing is off, a little bit of that energy disappears.

The Time & Place

If you're thinking of having your reception on the same day as the New York Marathon, the Pumpkin Festival in Half Moon Bay, SXSW in Austin, or JazzFest in New Orleans and you live in one of those cities, keep in mind that there will be thousands of people in town that day. And if any part of the big public event is near where your reception will be held, the parking and traffic will be nuts. A little advance research will save you and your guests a lot of frustration.

Check with your local chamber of commerce about events scheduled in the vicinity of your venue on the day of your wedding. You can even do an Internet search for your wedding date and the city of your venue to see if anything pops up. You may be surprised to find out about a parade, concert, sporting event, music festival, or other big event that's scheduled to take place very close to where you are going to be, especially if you are targeting the downtown area or a popular neighborhood.

If you have already booked the venue or still want to proceed, despite the competing event, warn your guests to expect traffic delays and/or limited parking. Give them options for routes to take and places to park. Make it easy for them. In some cases, you might even want to arrange for a shuttle for your guests. Annoying your guests before the wedding can carry right on through to the reception. Instead, we want them to be happy when they show up, with lots of positive energy.

The same idea applies if you are planning your wedding near the coast in the summer. Most likely there will be lots of people heading to the beach. Make sure you tell your guests to allow plenty of extra time to deal with the traffic. You may even want to travel there on the weekend to see how long it takes you to get from place to place. Then tell your guests! A simple reminder in the invitation is all that is needed. If you don't do this, you risk the chance of people arriving late, which can throw off the schedule for the entire afternoon or evening.

Although it's not always possible, try to avoid planning your wedding and reception on days that coincide with the World Series, the Super Bowl, or other major sporting events. Otherwise, the guys (and some women) at your reception may congregate in the bar to watch the game, instead of celebrating with you. If you can't avoid this overlap and there is a television at your reception location, make sure it is turned off. Arrange this with the coordinator of the facility ahead of time.

If you know you are going to have many sports fans in attendance, you can have the DJ or MC update the score during the reception to inject doses of energy into the gathering. Of course, with the way technology is these days, the guests will probably be getting their own updates on their cell phones anyway, so that may not be necessary — and it may not be a good idea if your local team is losing the game.

Before you finalize the date and book the venue, always check with the most important people on your guest list — your immediate family and bridal party members — to make sure they are available, just in case one of them has already paid for a big vacation for that day, has RSVP'd for another event, or has to be out of town on business.

Outdoor Receptions

Having your reception outside can be a wonderful experience for your guests. It can also be very uncomfortable, depending on the weather. Let your guests know ahead of time that they will be outdoors, then monitor the weather as the date approaches.

If it appears that it will be cold that day, make sure to arrange for outdoor heaters. If it is going to be a scorcher, set up protective umbrellas over every table. You may love the sun on your skin, but not everybody does. You may even want to provide a table with sunscreen, hand fans, and bottles of water or a water/lemonade station.

A few days before the reception, send out a reminder e-mail letting your guests know about the weather forecast and whether they need to bring jackets or hats and sunscreen.

Always have a backup plan in the event of rain. Many locations have an indoor room available, just in case. Otherwise, have a company on standby to erect a tent if one is needed. If the weather makes your guests uncomfortable, most likely they will not dance and they will probably leave early. And we don't want that!

By the way, for outdoor ceremonies in the summer, it is essential that you provide bottles of water or a water/lemonade station. Having guests suffer from thirst and overheating is no way to start off the day and can drain their energy. Setting up such a station doesn't cost much, and I consider this a must.

Room Layout

How you lay out the room can have an impact on the reception. Granted, at some locations, you may have absolutely no say in the matter — you need to do it their way or it's the highway. But if you have a choice, a room with a centrally located dance floor is always best.

If the dance floor is at one end of a long room, in a different room, or in an area where your guests can't see it, they will feel less connected, and that will bring the energy level down. If the dance floor is in the middle of the main or only room, the guests can see everything and can easily join in.

It's also best for the DJ and his speakers to be set up right next to the dance floor. That way, he can gauge the appropriate levels of sound for the dance floor, while keeping volume levels at the tables lower, allowing guests who aren't dancing to socialize.

If you must have a few tables between the speakers and the dance floor, make sure you do not seat the parents, grandparents, or senior guests at those tables. They will become annoyed with the sound level rather quickly. Instead, let some of your rowdier friends or maybe some of the kids sit there. They usually don't mind at all.

If your ballroom is long and rectangular and you have a large group, make sure your DJ positions an additional speaker or two on the other side or at least at the halfway point of the room, so the guests in the back can hear everything that's going on. Inexperienced DJ's will set up two speakers near where they are located and turn up the volume extra loud during the toasts and announcements so people in the back can hear, overwhelming the guests sitting at the tables that are closer to the speakers.

Bar Placement

If you can choose where the bar will be set up, make sure it is in the same room as the dinner and dancing; close to the dance floor is even better. If the venue you choose has a permanent bar in a different room, make sure the TV is turned off in that room, so people don't hang out there instead of in the main room. The DJ builds energy and creates a fun atmosphere by having as many of the guests in the room as possible.

Venues with Multiple Areas

I have DJ'd in some venues where the ceremony was in one area, the cocktails in another area, the dinner in another, the cake-cutting in another, and the dancing in another. My clients picked those venues because they were unique and had a variety of cool areas for hanging out, and they were able to utilize them all. The multiple areas may have even been what sold them on the place.

But a venue with too many rooms is one of the most difficult scenarios for a DJ to entertain in, since the party can become fragmented, with people spread out in the different locations. Sure, a cocktail hour is often held in a separate area, and that's okay. But if you want an exciting, high-energy reception, I strongly recommend having the dinner and dancing in the same room or area.

Let's say you are thinking about doing the cake-cutting outside and serving the slices of cake to the guests there. If it's a beautiful afternoon or evening, they may not come back for a while. Some may even hang out there for the whole reception, drinking and chatting. That's okay if you are planning a laid-back reception and dancing is not important to you. But if that's the case, you probably wouldn't be reading this book.

Most people want a fun, upbeat reception with lots of dancing. If the dancing and dinner are going to be in separate areas, make sure you do the cake-cutting in the room or area where the dancing will happen. In that area, give the guests a place to put their personal things and a place to eat the cake without having to go back to the dining room. Once they leave the dancing area to go back to the dining room for the cake-cutting, it can be very difficult to get them to come back.

Remember: In most cases, less is more. Guests can also get tired of going back and forth, wondering if they should leave their purses or personal belongings in one area while they go to another area. Keep it simple.

DIYers

You may be so excited about your wedding day that you feel like doing everything yourself. Don't. You should ask for help. Why? Trying to do everything causes stress, and too much stress will overwhelm you.

Please don't think you need to prove to yourself, your fiancé, your parents, or anyone else that you can do everything yourself (even if think you can). Ask for help. You'll be surprised by how many people would love to help and how much more enjoyable the planning will be. That being said, don't let anyone pressure you into using their help. Choose wisely!

The Overbearing Mother-in-Law

Do you have an overbearing mother-in-law? Is she butting in and already dictating how she thinks the wedding day should unfold? Let me tell you something very important: The problem isn't your mother-in-law. I'm serious. The problem is . . . your fiancé. You heard me. Your fiancé is obviously not standing up to her and putting her in her place. Your fiancé needs to back you up. With your fiancé, it's two against one and you win. Without your fiancé, you lose.

Let me say that again and use a boldface font for emphasis:

Your fiancé needs to back you 100 percent of the time.

You need to cut off an overbearing mother quickly or she will make not only your wedding but your life a living hell. If you don't, your mother-in-law has the power. And *you* have the stress.

An over-bearing mother-in-law is a surefire way to bring more stress into your wedding planning — and into your life — along with many, many, many tears. I've had more than one bride cry during one of our consultations because her mother-in-law was dictating how everything would go on the wedding day. Tell me, whose wedding is it?

I'll repeat: You need complete support from your fiancé. This is one of the most important pieces of advice I can give you regarding the wedding planning. Sit down with your partner in the beginning stages to talk about what things are most important to you and the things you will not budge on. Of course, you should listen to your fiancé's needs as well.

Remember: This advice applies not only to your wedding, but to the rest of your life. If your mother-in-law is not cut off now, she will probably be happy to tell you in the future where you should live, how to raise your kids, what diapers they should wear, how to wipe their butts, and so much more. Cut her off now.

An Overbearing Mom

Yes, I've seen a whole bunch of overbearing moms too. The usual line from her is, "Hey, I'm paying for this wedding, so I have a say in what's going to happen." Cut her off as well. Obviously, you are not going to be rude about it. But it needs to be done.

If she threatens to not pay for the wedding, then you have to make a decision. Is it worth all the stress and tears? Planning the wedding is supposed to be fun. Cut her off. You may say, "Rich, she is paying for the entire wedding; I can't do that." Okay, then you need to decide what things you are okay in giving in on.

Make a list of all the things that need to be done, the things you don't mind giving up control over. But she should have no say whatsoever in who is going to be in your bridal party, what your colors will be, what will be said in the ceremony, and choosing your First Dance song. Send her the list of the tasks that need to be done; let her know that you are dividing them between a few people and that she can pick a few things from the list to help out with, if she wants.

Overbearing parents may also give you a list (sometimes longer than your entire guest list) of people they think you should or must invite. There is a good chance you won't even know some of those people. Take a stand. Find a number that is reasonable for you and tell your parents they can invite that many people.

You are not having a celebrity wedding and inviting everyone, including the paparazzi. If you see that your mother or mother-in-law is going to be overbearing, sit down with her at the beginning of the planning and let her know that planning the reception is the first important thing that you and your future spouse will be doing together. It's important that you do it by yourselves. Tell her she just needs to show up and enjoy the party. Having this conversation early in the planning is important.

Hiring the DJ

Nothing is as important as the DJ at a wedding reception. Nothing!

You may be saying, "Rich, what about the food?" Well, the food *is* important. But a bad DJ will give your guests indigestion and send them running for the exits well before your scheduled ending time.

A bad DJ will embarrass you by mispronouncing your names during your Grand Introduction and by using highly sophisticated language like "Yo Yo Yo" and "Wusssssup." I've heard stories of the photographer not capturing photos of the First Dance because the DJ failed to make sure she was in the room before he started playing the song. And of DJ's who played the *wrong* song for the First Dance. How sad.

There are thousands of websites offering advice on how to hire a DJ, so I won't spend a lot of time on this. But I will try to give you a different perspective.

If you've already hired a DJ, that's great. Just pick out the things in this book that resonate with you and let him know you would like to incorporate them into your reception program. Don't assume he knows most of this stuff and will do it without you asking.

And I am not suggesting that the only way you will have a good time at your wedding reception is to hire a DJ. No! I have been to a few weddings with live bands that were amazing. So if you are going to hire a band (or already have), that's great. Just make sure they have an articulate band member who can act as the MC. If not, hire an MC separately. Or you can hire a DJ/MC to make all the announcements and play music during the twenty-minute band breaks every hour.

But back to our main subject: If you do want a DJ and haven't yet hired one, the top two things to look for when hiring a DJ are personality and experience.

Personality

This is number one — even more important than experience, which I'll discuss next. The DJ will be representing you in front of your friends and families. Make sure he has a personality you like. You can get a good feel for a DJ's personality by reading his blog, if he has one. If he doesn't have one, meet him person. If, during your consultation, he never smiles, and you are looking for someone cheerful and positive, do not hire him. If your potential DJ jokes around a lot and does all the talking and you are looking for someone low-key and elegant, do not hire him.

Find a DJ with a personality that you connect with because you are going to see *that* personality at your reception.

Before you make a decision on who is the best fit for you, meet at least three DJ's in person to get a feel for their personalities and how they present themselves.

Experience

This is a big one too. A highly experienced DJ will not only be able to read the crowd and play the right songs at the right time; he will also know what to do when he encounters an empty dance floor after playing a song that you specifically requested but that bombed (I'll talk more later about choosing your songs wisely). He'll know how to make adjustments to the schedule when things get off track because of, say, a ceremony that went too long or a dinner that was not ready to be served at the scheduled time.

Now that we've established personality and experience as the two most essential qualities for the person who will run your wedding reception, here are a few other considerations as you search for a DJ.

Price

When budgeting for a DJ, some people just make up a number like $600 or $800 because it sounds good to them. That is a huge mistake, especially if the average price for a DJ in your area is $1,200. If that's the case, you are going to end up with a DJ who is way below par.

You can't come up with a budget for your DJ until you know the average price for a DJ in your area. And beware of using a budget guide that you found online that tells you what you should pay for a DJ. Those are absolutely ridiculous, in my opinion, because a DJ could cost twice or three times as much in San Francisco or New York as a DJ in Walla Walla, Washington (yes, that's a real city).

After you have found several DJ's with personalities you connect with and the amount of experience you feel comfortable with, you can compare their prices and see which one you gravitate toward as you balance your preference with their prices.

Award-Winning or Fancy-Titled DJ's

You do not need to hire an "award-winning" or a "certified" DJ in order to have an incredible wedding reception. That may seem like odd advice from a guy who has won "Best DJ in Silicon Valley" two years in a row. But it's true, and I want to be honest with you.

I have some DJ friends who have *never* won a single award, and they are amazing DJ's and I would hire them in a heartbeat.

Some website awards are bogus anyway, in my opinion. I've seen some DJ's who have received "Best Of" or "Bride's Choice" and then noticed that so did all the other active paid advertisers on those websites. Seems a little fishy, right?

Some websites and publications let people vote for their favorite DJ's, but usually the winners are DJ's who have e-mailed every friend, relative, acquaintance, strangers they met at the airport, and past clients multiple times, asking them to vote for them on a particular website. The majority of the votes may not even come from past clients. They've posted on Facebook "Vote for Me!" and some even say you can vote more than once! They are not really the best DJ, are they? They are just the ones who were able to get the most people to vote for them. Of course, this is different than being voted the winner of an award from your peers in an organization or industry.

A DJ Who Is Familiar with Your Venue

Many wedding resources, books, and websites suggest you find out if your potential DJ has been to your venue, because they consider it a plus. I don't agree with this at all.

It's not that big of a deal if the DJ has never been to your wedding venue, as long as you meet him there to do a site walk-through ahead of time. Yes, I've booked many jobs because the client knew I was familiar with their venue. But there are some venues I had never been to and I was still able to deliver the same top service that my clients expect from me.

Bottom line: Don't make this a big factor in considering a DJ. Just make sure the DJ sees the venue before the wedding day, and you'll be fine.

An Owner-Operated DJ Company vs. a Multi-DJ Company

Even though I personally have an owner-operated DJ company, I still have no problem recommending a company with multiple DJ's. Most owner-operated DJ companies will argue that you can't get outstanding, personalized customer service with a big DJ company. This is simply not true.

Although not all DJ companies are created equal, I do know several companies with multiple DJ's in my area that I would feel 100 percent comfortable recommending. Of course, they are the ones that have an actual physical office with someone there during the day who is easily accessible.

Be careful with companies that have multiple DJ's but that do not have a physical office or are located in another state. It's possible they are just companies that book jobs and then subcontract them out to DJ's in your area. One of the best ways to see how they operate is to ask if you can meet the potential DJ ahead of time, before you sign the contract. If they say no . . . run.

The argument that some larger DJ companies use against an owner-operated company is that since there is only one DJ in the company, they don't have backup resources if he gets sick or has some kind of crisis. This is also ridiculous. A professional DJ who cares about the reputation of his company and about offering excellent customer service will always have backup equipment and a couple of backup DJ's he can call on at a moment's notice, in case of an emergency. Just ask. And get it in writing.

Chapter Two

The Schedule of Events

You've most likely been to several wedding receptions where the events were very similar. But not every reception is equal.

More Is Not Always Better

The first principle of planning a successful program for your wedding reception is to not include too many events. That can be a little overwhelming for the guests. They need some breathing room to socialize and actually enjoy the event. You don't have to entertain them every minute of every hour.

Some couples are paranoid that their guests are going to be bored, so they overplan and organize too many activities. On the other end of the spectrum are those who schedule too much time between activities so the guests actually do become bored as they wait for the next activity to happen. You need to find the balance.

This is where an experienced DJ comes into play. Someone who has DJ'd many receptions will be likely to do a good job in moving yours along at a comfortable pace.

Deciding What to Include

The number and type of events, and how long each event will last, will vary depending on the size of the guest list and the goals of the bride and groom.

If the goal is lots of socializing, the cocktail hour can be closer to ninety minutes, instead of the usual sixty. The dinner can run longer too. This is very common at traditional Chinese receptions, which normally include nine courses during a three-hour culinary extravaganza. The food keeps coming and coming and coming! It's a wonderful experience, but it is not for everybody. Most wedding meals last between seventy-five and ninety minutes.

A typical wedding reception program includes several optional events — the blessing, special dances, and a video or slideshow. The bouquet and garter toss can be considered optional as well; not every couple wants to include them.

Here is the typical order of the events, and their timing, for a five-hour reception:

Cocktails/Appetizers: 60 minutes

Guests Invited into Ballroom: (enter and find seats) 10 minutes

Grand Entrance: 5 minutes

First Dance: (bride & groom) 3.5 minutes

Toasts: Best Man, Maid of Honor, Father of the Bride, Father of the Groom…..5 minutes per person = 20 minutes

(*Optional*) Blessing: 2 minutes

Meal: 60-75 minutes

(*Optional*) Video Presentation / Slide Show: 8-10 minutes

Father-Daughter Dance: 3.5 minutes

Groom-Mother Dance: 3.5 minutes

Open Dancing: (first set) 20-40 minutes

Cake-Cutting: 5 minutes

Bouquet & Garter: 5 minutes each

Open Dancing: (second set) 45-75 minutes

Last Dance: 3.5 minutes

The Big Send-Off: (optional) 5 minutes

The cocktail hour is typically the first event your guests will experience when they arrive at the reception venue after the ceremony (unless, of course, you are having the ceremony on the same property).

Most often, the bride and groom will be off taking post-ceremony photos with the bridal party. If that's not the case or if the photographer finishes before the end of the cocktail hour, you may wonder whether you should join in or wait for the Grand

Introduction. Some couples believe the bride and groom should not be seen until the Grand Entrance, so they avoid entering the cocktail area, but that doesn't have to be the case.

You'll already be married, and seeing you at the cocktail hour won't make it any less exciting or dramatic for the guests when you are introduced during the Grand Entrance. If you're available, I strongly encourage you to join the guests during the cocktail hour. This is a great time for you to socialize with them, exchange hugs and kisses, and start celebrating. Your wedding day happens only once, so you should enjoy as much time as possible with your friends and family.

If you greet and chat with people before the meal, you can spend less time mingling with them after dinner, which means you will have more time for dancing. This is especially helpful when you are planning a shorter reception.

The list of events and timing given above is for a five-hour reception. If you're planning a six-hour reception, just add an extra hour of open dancing.

You will have more time for dancing if you have a smaller guest list (the dinner will be served faster) or, for larger guest lists, if you arrange for a two-sided buffet so the wait time is much shorter. I cover this, along with some other timesaving tricks, in Chapter Five: The Meal.

You can also create more time for dancing by planning for fewer or shorter toasts, skipping the video/slideshow or playing it on a loop during the cocktail hour, or by combining the Father-Bride and Groom-Mother dances into just one song for both.

You'll notice that I recommend doing your First Dance directly after the Grand Introduction. This is an easy way to instantly create more energy, since most of the guests don't expect it to happen so quickly. I recommend it to all my clients. This timing is also ideal for the bride and groom who are nervous about dancing and want to get it out of the way.

If things are running late and you risk the chance of the food getting cold or dried out or if you know that you and your guests will be starving, make sure everyone gets their food first, before you get into the toasts. You can even have the DJ or MC announce that it's okay for everyone to enjoy their meals while the toasts are going on. Or you can just wait until everyone is almost finished eating before proceeding with the toasts.

One thing that is very common and takes a lot of time is the bride and groom going table to table to say hello to all of the guests after the meal. This mingling can easily eat up thirty to sixty minutes of your dancing time, depending on the number of tables at your reception. And the guests on the other side of the room may get bored as they wait for you to come their way.

To avoid this scenario, socialize with your guests during the cocktail hour. Yes, this is typically when the formal photos are taken with the bridal party and family members. So that means you would need to do many of the formal photos with the bridal party and family before the ceremony. (If the bride and groom don't want to see each other before the ceremony, obviously this will not work.)

Another option is to not give the photographer a crazy-long list of required photos, so you can get the formal photos done more quickly and join the guests during the second half of the cocktail hour. You can also mingle with them while they are eating cake or while you are dancing with them.

Why Wedding Receptions Fall Behind Schedule

There are lots of reasons why a reception might fall behind schedule, but these are the most common problems:

* The ceremony started late.

* The photos following the ceremony took too long.

* The toasts took too long.

* It's an outdoor reception and it started to rain.

* The meal wasn't ready at the specified time.

* There were many guests and the dinner buffet was one-sided instead of two-sided.

* The bride and groom took too long mingling with each table after the meal.

* The photographer took the bride and groom away from the reception to take sunset photos.

Any one of these possibilities can bring down the energy level of the reception, throw the schedule off, make the guests antsy, restless, or bored (or all of the above), and eat up time the guests could spend dancing.

When I mention delay problems that are related to the photos, I am not saying that it is necessarily the photographer's fault. Family members can wander away from the photo area, despite being asked to stay close by, or the bride and groom may have drawn up an unbelievably long list of photos.

If the bride and groom do not want to see each other before the ceremony, that is fine. But the photographer can still shoot photos of just the bride, just the groom, just the bridesmaids, and just the groomsmen . . . all before the ceremony. Doing this saves time.

Chapter Three

The Grand Entrance

As festive as the cocktail hour can be, it's the Grand Entrance that really gets the party going. It can be one of the most exciting and exhilarating moments of your day. This is where an experienced MC with the right personality comes into play. You want someone who can deliver a lively introduction that can also be fun, creative, and humorous.

There's one very important thing to remember in order to have a successful Grand Entrance: Go over the pronunciations of all names with the DJ ahead of time — not at the reception!

Everything should be personal; always use first names. For instance, we would never say, "It's time for the bride and groom to cut the cake." It's much better to say, "It's time for Billy and Susie to cut the cake." A lot of DJ's don't do this, so you would be wise to make it clear to your DJ that you prefer to be called by your first names, instead of "the bride and groom." You may also want to write the introductions yourself if you are not confident of your DJ's ability.

Making Introductions

There are several options for the Grand Entrance, depending on the personalities of the bride and groom.

Bride & Groom Only

The most basic of all introductions involves just the bride and the groom. Still, it can be fun for both of you as your guests stand and greet you with cheers as you enter the room to one of your favorite songs. Pick out a fun song and enjoy! If you are using first and last names and the bride will take the groom's last name, I recommend putting the bride's name second, after the groom's, so everyone can hear her first name next to her new last name:

Jim and Stacy Blackford!

or

The All-New Mr. and Mrs. Blackford!

Parents & Bridal Party

In the most popular introduction, your DJ or MC introduces your parents, the bridal party, and you by your first and last names. Your bridal party can enter in pairs or one person at a time. Have the DJ play one of your favorite upbeat songs, and enjoy the experience as everyone welcomes you into the room like rock stars. It's simple and straightforward, yet fun.

Please welcome the Maid of Honor and the Best Man . . . Ashley Jacobi and Bill Struts!

The bridal party can have some fun with this one too and show some personality: bust a move, swing your partner, slap him on the buns, whatever you want. But if you have a *really* outgoing bridal party, you may want to have them do "Top That!"

Top That!

If your bridal party is playful (and maybe a little competitive), this is a simple yet fun way to give them a moment in the limelight. The basic idea is that each couple tries to top the last couple's dance moves.

You can use the same song for everyone or switch it up and play a different song for each couple. Only about thirty seconds of each song is needed, so make sure the DJ cues up the song at the chorus so the guests hear the most recognizable part of the song.

"Top That!" is a lot of fun and can get a little crazy, with some people trying to imitate Vanilla Ice or MC Hammer. I've even seen a groomsman pick up a bridesmaid over his head and spin her around as if they were performing on *So You Think You Can Dance?*

My Boogie Shoes

Looking for something silly and fun? One of my clients did this, and I thought it was pretty funny. The bride surprised all the members of the bridal party by giving them each a wacky pair of fuzzy, colorful, animal slippers, and they all danced their way into the ballroom to the song "Boogie Shoes" by KC and the Sunshine Band. You could tell they really enjoyed it, and the guests were laughing, which is always a good thing.

And Now . . . Your Wedding All-Stars!

This is a high-energy introduction that is a lot of fun and takes the energy to the next level. Have your MC introduce you and the members of the bridal party as though they are professional athletes at the big game. Make sure you pick out an up-tempo song to go along with this!

> *Starting at ring bearer and tipping the scales at whopping 44 pounds, a graduate of Blue Hills Pre-School, Johnny Garcia!*

Introductions with Bios

This is top-level fun and will get a whole bunch of laughs too. Plus, it's a big surprise for your bridal party members since they don't know you are doing this! Shhh. It's a surprise! You can write these bios yourself, or if you have an experienced DJ or MC with a personality, give him the necessary information and have him write it.

Here's the kind of info you can use to compile a fun introduction for each member of the bridal party:

* Occupation
* Hobbies

* What they are most known for

* Bad or weird habits

* Relation to the bride or groom: Where did they meet? How long have they known each other?

* Where would you most likely find them on a Saturday night?

* Favorite restaurant or food or snack or drink

* Are they obsessed with anything? Any gadget? Any sports team? Any odd TV show or cartoon?

* Any other useful info

Give as much dirt as possible for each member of the bridal party without revealing anything too personal or information that might embarrass them. The DJ or MC does not have to use all of these. Just use the fun, unique, or impressive things, and forget the rest. For example, one of my clients gave me the following info about one of the groomsmen, Zach:

* Zach is a graduate of San Jose State.

* He loves Sudoku and beer pong.

* He is an awesome yoga instructor.

That wasn't really a lot to work with, but using a little creativity, I came up with something fun that the guests (and Zach himself) really loved. Here's what I wrote and delivered:

A graduate of San Jose State, where he majored in beer pong and Sudoku, this very *flexible man is known as one of the top yoga instructors in Silicon Valley and is probably the only person here today who can scratch the back of his neck with his toes. Give it up for Zach Armstrong!*

See how easy it can be? Then you just take what you have and add some fun music. These bios don't have to be long at all. In fact, keep them on the shorter side if you have a big bridal party. But just a few short sentences can add a whole bunch of fun and energy to your reception!

The Parents

A lot of couples don't know whether to introduce their parents along with the bridal party. If you have fun or outgoing parents or if you want to make them feel special, I highly recommend it. They will enjoy the spotlight, and it will be a special moment for them as well.

If your parents are a little more on the conservative side, that's okay. The DJ or MC can acknowledge them and they can just stand up from their tables and wave to everyone.

Divorced Parents

It's perfectly okay for divorced parents to come in with the Grand Entrance. If one of them does not have a new spouse or significant other, you can pair them up with another family member or the flower girl or ring bearer. The same goes for stepparents. Let's say, for example, that the groom's name is Billy. Following are some examples for how to introduce Billy's divorced parents.

If Billy's father has a girlfriend:

> *Please welcome Billy's father, John Johnson, accompanied by Jill Cardoza.*

Notice how we did not say "his girlfriend." That's not necessary and may sound awkward to some people. (Billy's mother probably wouldn't like it all that much, for example.)

If Billy's parents are divorced and the mom has no current significant other, pair her up with another family member and say something like this:

> *Please welcome Billy's mother, Valerie Johnson, escorted by her nephew, Steve VanGough!*

If Billy's father has remarried:

> *Please welcome Billy's father, John Johnson, and his wife, Jill.*

If your parents are divorced and can't stand to be in the presence of one another (yes, I've encountered this a few times), just acknowledge them individually from their tables; that will be fine and should not ruffle any feathers. Please understand that it is also perfectly fine *not* to introduce them at all. This is a personal preference, so do whatever you and your parents feel most comfortable with.

Finally, if you have a special relationship with your grandparents and think the world of them, make sure you introduce them.

Music Suggestions for the Grand Entrance

This song is important, so choose it wisely. My best advice is make it fun and make it upbeat! You can do a particular movie theme, such as the music from *Star Wars* or *Rocky*, or maybe a game show theme, or just choose a popular song that will get the guests clapping their hands as you enter the room. It could be an older classic or a current song that's played on the radio today. Here are a few of the most popular songs for the Grand Entrance:

"Gonna Fly Now" (theme from *Rocky*) by Bill Conti

"Star Wars" (main theme)" by John Williams

"Celebration" by Kool & the Gang

"Beautiful Day" by U2

"Thunderstruck" by AC/DC (This one is very popular at sporting events and really rocks!)

"This Will Be (an Everlasting Love)" by Natalie Cole (The ladies love this one)

"Eye of the Tiger" by Survivor

"I Gotta Feeling" by the Black Eyed Peas

"Now That We Found Love" by Heavy D & the Boyz

"Good Life" by OneRepublic

"Signed, Sealed, Delivered, I'm Yours" by Stevie Wonder

"You Make My Dreams Come True" by Hall & Oates

"Get Ready for This" by 2 Unlimited

"Another One Bites the Dust" by Queen

"Walking on Sunshine" by Katrina and the Waves

"Sirius" by the Alan Parsons Project

"We Are Family" by Sister Sledge

"You're the First, the Last, My Everything" by Barry White

"The Way You Make Me Feel" by Michael Jackson

"Get the Party Started" by Pink

"Viva la Vida" by Coldplay

Chapter Four

The Toasts

Toasts are a very important part of the festivities and can really be fun and emotional. But long, drawn-out toasts can kill the energy in the room. And that's the last thing we want since we are trying to build energy and momentum leading up to the dancing.

There's another important consideration: The caterer needs to time the meal, starting with the appetizers. Food is a huge expense, and it makes no sense to hire a great caterer if you're going to tie his hands by not sticking to the schedule. Most caterers can work around a five- or ten-minute delay. But give them a twenty-to-thirty-minute delay and you may have a ruined meal. It is crucial that the people offering the toasts understand this.

If because of the number of people offering toasts or the personalities of the individuals involved, you fear that the timeline may suffer, I recommend that you have the caterer serve the food before the toasts begin. It's no big deal to delay the toasts. It *is* a big deal if the chicken tastes like cardboard.

Prep your toasters a few weeks before the reception, letting them know that they need to keep their toasts to a maximum of five minutes each. If they are using notes, ask them to practice at home, out loud, to get the timing right. Short, sweet, and humorous toasts are ideal.

And if one of the groomsmen is a little on the wild side and the thought of him with a microphone gives you hives, you may want to have your fiancé chat with him about what you feel is appropriate and inappropriate so he doesn't embarrass you or make Grandma Betty pass out.

Open Mic

Offering the microphone to the rest of the guests (after the formal toasts have finished) can be fun because of the off-the-cuff, spontaneous words that are likely to flow from the toasters' lips. Of course, this can also backfire and you may be subjecting your guests to someone who makes a fool of himself or says something completely inappropriate. If you have a fun, outgoing guest list of family and friends, it may work. But it may not. You need to make the call on that.

An open mic session also has a tendency to run long, though, so it is not recommended if you have a tight schedule and/or limited time for dancing.

The Order of Toasts

When it comes to the order of the toasts, there really aren't rules anymore. Don't put too much thought into the order, unless you know someone is going to be super-creative and funny. If that's the case, save that person for last so you end with a bang.

Thank You!

It's a very nice gesture for the bride and groom to toast the guests and thank them for coming to celebrate with them. This is usually done at the beginning of the meal, or at the end of the formal toasts, or toward the end of the meal, or after the cake-cutting. It's a great opportunity to thank those guests who have traveled long distances to celebrate with you or to honor others who could not make it, have passed away, or are celebrating a birthday or anniversary.

If the thought of being on the microphone makes your skin crawl, no big deal. You can just have the MC or a family member say a few words on your behalf.

Table Toasts

These are very popular at Asian weddings, and I really like them, because they can be memorable and fun for the bride and groom (and the guests).

It might seem that doing toasts at each table would be time-consuming, but they can be done remarkably quickly. If you had plans for mingling and going to each table to say hello to the guests, but the schedule has been compromised or you're afraid you won't have a lot of time for dancing, do table toasts instead. They don't eat up as much time as mingling — it takes just one minute per table to raise your glass and salute the people who came to celebrate with you. The guests will enjoy it, and then you can quickly move on to the next table.

Make sure you tell the photographer you are going to do this. It can be nice for them to follow the bride and groom from table to table to snap a shot of each toast.

Chapter Five

The Meal

This may seem silly to say, but you need to sit down and eat your meal. This is your first meal together as a married couple, and it's a very special moment.

I'm always surprised by how many newlyweds feel obligated to mingle and chat with their guests during the meal. You don't need to do this! They will be fine without you. Plus, when you talk to them during the dinner, *their* food gets cold because they feel uncomfortable stuffing their faces while you are visiting with them.

You're going to need all the energy you can muster to get through the rest of the reception, so sit down, take a deep breath, and relax. Really take in the moment as you witness your friends and family celebrating this special day with you. Feel the love. Feel the gratitude. Eat your meal. Save your mingling for later.

Speaking of mingling, there are certain points throughout the reception that can be set aside for spending quality time with your guests. You should have time to circulate among your guests toward the end of meal since the bridal party is served prior to the guests, leaving you time to mix and mingle with the crowd as they finish up their meals.

Likewise, if you are having a buffet, you and the bridal party will get your food first and thus you will finish the meal first. Then you can start mingling with the people at the tables that got their food right after you, since they will be the next ones to finish.

An important pointer: You need to monitor the amount of time you will spend mingling. Think of it this way: If you had 180 people at your reception and spent just one minute saying hello to each one, it would take three hours! If your time is limited but you still feel you have to mingle, have your more intimate chats with the people who traveled from out of town first, or those you don't see very often. You can save the more informal greetings for your coworkers and the friends you see on a regular basis.

Better yet, talk to each table as a group, if possible, and save all the hugs and kisses for later when everyone is up and dancing or at the bar.

Table-Hopping & Eating

I remember the first time one of my clients did this — I thought it was the coolest idea. The bride and groom knew that they weren't going to have much time to mingle with everyone during the reception so they set up two extra chairs at each table. On the table, in front of those chairs, was a sign that said, "RESERVED FOR THE BRIDE AND GROOM." Then, once the dinner started, they table-hopped!

They literally grabbed their dinner plates and sat down at each table for five minutes to visit with the guests! Then after a little bit of chatting and a few bites of food with one table, they got up and headed to the next table to do the same thing. This really kept the energy level up in the room and was *a lot* of fun for the guests.

Table Names

I can't believe people still do table numbers! Let me spell this one out for you . . . B-O-R-I-N-G! My wife and I named our tables after places we had visited while we were dating. You can even place on each table a photo of the two of you when you were at that location. This adds so much more personality to the table and gives your guests something to talk about!

Not into traveling? How about table names with your favorite TV shows or movies or wines or animals? You get the idea. Something as simple as naming your tables creatively adds energy to the reception.

Cigars, Cigarettes & Outside Smoking

At a wedding I DJ'd a few years ago, the groom was a big-time cigar aficionado. He brought a bunch of boxes of cigars to the reception. After dinner, he had me announce that anyone who wanted to join him on the patio for a stogie should go there. I had a bad feeling about that one, and I was right. A few seconds later, the ballroom was a ghost town as 80 percent of the guys (and some women) left the ballroom to join him outside. They did not return for more than two hours, and that cigar-focused interlude pretty much killed the reception inside.

Just remember, if you give people a reason to leave the ballroom or dancing area, some of them will probably do just that (and they may not come back).

If you or your fiancé smokes cigarettes, try to limit the times you run outside to smoke because it has an impact on the timing, flow, and energy of the reception — especially since you will most likely draw people out of the room with you. If you are heavy smokers, you should allow extra time in your schedule for the smoke breaks you think you will be taking.

The Buffet Meal

If you are going to have a buffet, ask your caterers if they can set up a two-sided buffet. This arrangement gets your guests through the buffet faster and gives you more time for dancing later. If you have a large guest list, you may need to have the DJ or MC play some games or trivia contests with the guests so people don't get bored while waiting to grab their food.

Food Stations

While not always practical (depending on the size and layout of the room), food stations are a great way to add fun and energy to a reception. They get everyone up and moving around, which is the complete opposite of a stuffy reception. You can have a pasta station and a sushi station and a taco bar . . . you get the idea.

Caffeine? Yes, Please!

This could be one of the most important parts of the dinner. You know how you can get sluggish sometimes after a meal? The last thing you want is for your guests to be dragging. Make sure you have the coffee and tea flowing after dinner.

And you don't have to wait for the cake to have it available. In fact, the easiest thing to do is to have a coffee station that's available for your guests at any time. Have the DJ or MC announce that it is there. You can even take it to another level and pamper your guests with a professionally catered espresso bar that offers an alternative to the coffee that's typically served. Of course, if budget is a factor, just regular coffee will do and will be perfectly fine and very much appreciated. This is a must.

Your Vendors Are Starving!

Don't forget to arrange meals for your vendors. They are working hard for you and don't take breaks.

It's common for some photographers to start shooting in the morning, as you are getting ready for the ceremony, and to not stop until the end of the reception. That can be twelve to fourteen hours!

If you are going to have a buffet, let your vendors go through the buffet line right after the bridal party and family members go through, so they can eat quickly and be ready for anything that happens. This is especially important if your photographer is going to be following you around from table to table while you mingle with the guests.

And don't forget to include the vendors in the meal count, and make sure the caterer knows about the plan. For sit-down dinners, you can arrange for a separate table for the vendors in the corner. Some facilities also offer special vendor meals at a reduced rate. You should decide if the meals offered are sufficient for your vendors or if you want them to eat the same food as the guests (sometimes the vendor meals are just a boxed lunch with a cold sandwich, potato chips, an apple, and a cookie). Although I am not picky at all when it comes to food (I am just happy to be getting something!), I hear wedding vendors complain about this all the time.

Make sure to check if your vendors have any dietary restrictions — for example, if they are vegetarians. Keep your vendors happy, and they will have lots of energy to perform at optimum levels.

Sunset Photos

Photographers often want to steal the bride and groom away from the reception to go outside and take sunset photos. This is a perfectly fine idea. Just don't do it when the dancing is getting ready to start or just after it begins.

It is very important for the bride and groom to be on the dance floor when the dancing begins (even if you don't like dancing). Why? Because the guests feed off your energy. You set the example, so try to make it a good one.

Your guests want to celebrate with you. If you are not in the room when the dancing begins, that can bring down the energy in the room and be a cause for them to leave early. Try your best to be on the dance floor for the first three songs of the open dancing. After that, you are off the hook. This is typically more difficult for the groom than it is for the bride, since women tend to dance more than men.

If the dancing is about to start but it's also the perfect time for sunset photos, go take the sunset photos if they are that important to you. Just don't dawdle, and delay the start of dancing until after you get back. Trust me on this one.

Chapter Six

The Music

It's a great idea to have lively music planned throughout all the events of your reception to set the mood for your guests.

Cocktail & Dinner Music

If you have live entertainment scheduled for the cocktail hour, that's excellent; it adds a ton of personality to your reception.

If your DJ is providing the music for the cocktail hour, that's great too. Just make sure he stays away from classical music! I know some people think it is elegant because they saw it once in a movie. But classical music is low energy, and you want to *build* the energy. And what are the chances that your guests will sway back and forth and tap their toes to a classical song from Bach or Beethoven during the cocktail hour? Sure, it's possible, but it's not very likely.

But what if you have some cool mid-tempo music or love songs from the '60's, '70's, '80's, or '90's that your guests will recognize, or popular jazz vocal standards from Frank Sinatra, Dean Martin, and Michael Bublé? You can be sure they will enjoy that!

The cocktail hour and dinner can also be a great time to have the DJ play some of the songs you love that aren't so danceable. Do you have a fiancé who likes only heavy-metal music? No problem. Find the most mellow heavy-metal songs from his favorite artists and sprinkle a couple in. It totally works! Do you love country music but know most of your guests don't like it or won't dance to it? No problem! Mix some in during the cocktail hour and dinner.

It is especially important to play your favorite non-danceable songs during times when people are either standing around drinking or seated, instead of during the dancing; otherwise, you will clear the dance floor. Make sure the music is not too loud, though. You want people to drink and socialize. That's what makes it fun. Everyone speaking in raised voices gets annoying after a while, and your guests may try to escape to another area for some peace and quiet — which is not what you want.

Looking for something more hip and exotic? Try some cool Spanish flamenco guitar. I recommend going to iTunes or to Amazon.com and listen to samples so you can pick out music you like.

Open Dancing

Now comes the time many people have been waiting for . . . the dancing! Let the fun begin! If you've kept your guests engaged and entertained and well-lubricated, they are most likely going to sprint to the dance floor to bust a move (unless you've picked obscure music that you think is cool but nobody else likes).

Has this happened in my experience? Oh, you bet! I've even tried to talk clients out of playing a certain type of music because I knew (based on other receptions I'd DJ'd) that it usually doesn't work. Most listen, though some don't. The ones that don't usually run up to me during the reception (after seeing the empty dance floor) and tell me that they've changed their minds and want me to play something that will get everybody to dance.

Open dancing is not the time to "show off" your eclectic music tastes. If you just have to do that, do it during the dinner or cocktail hour. To get the maximum number of people onto the dance floor, play popular, danceable music that everyone recognizes. Playing an entire afternoon or evening of rap and hip-hop or indie or techno music *will not work*, unless every single person happens to be into that music (something that is very rare).

Do your best to take into the consideration the likes and dislikes of your parents, your friends, the grandparents, and everyone else before coming up with a list of preferred songs and genres.

#1 Tip for Dancing

To repeat: You both really should be on the dance floor when open dancing starts. In doing so, you set a good example, as your guests will want to celebrate with you. Remember: They feel your energy.

When the dancing begins, I recommend that you both stay out there for at least three fast songs. Most of my clients love to dance, so this is usually not an issue. Still, I tell all my clients this. It's important, especially when you have guests who are conservative.

Speaking of which, you can take your encouragement one step further and grab someone out of their seat, saying, "I want to dance with you!" In fact, make sure you tell the bridal party that you need their help and would like to have them on the dance floor with you for the first few songs of open dancing, to really get things going. This will motivate others to get out there with you since some people don't like to be the first ones on the dance floor. I'll repeat: For the best results, *you* should set a good example and be out there on the dance floor.

Do I guarantee everyone will rush out onto the dance floor? Of course not. No DJ can guarantee that because not all guest lists are alike. You may have a very conservative guest list (which could include the members in your bridal party), so the DJ may have to pull a couple of tricks out of his sleeve to get the party started. Here are a few possibilities.

The Group Photo Trick

Have the DJ or MC ask *everyone* to come to the dance floor to join you for a group photo. After the photo is taken, have him ask everyone to stay right where they are because "the newlyweds" want to share a couple of special songs with everyone. If there are lots of couples, play a slow song. If there are lots of single people, have the DJ play something upbeat and fun.

It's best to start off with a classic song from the past that everyone will know. That way, the parents and grandparents will be motivated to stay out there too since the song will be familiar to them. If the majority of your guests are on younger side, start with a current radio hit. This should break the ice and get everyone going.

The group photo can also work later in the reception if things have slowed down and there isn't as much dancing going on.

OMG! Nobody Is Dancing!

If people just won't get their buns out of their seats at your reception, no matter what the DJ plays, have him start playing slow romantic songs. Even if most of the guests in your group are not big dancers, most likely they have a few romantic bones in their bodies and will at least get up to dance to a slow song with their spouse.

I once had a reception like that and I ended up playing eight or nine slow songs in a row. And the dance floor was packed for every song! Then I tried a fast song and everyone disappeared. It was a ghost town — I think I even heard crickets! — so I went back to playing slow songs, and everyone was happy. Needing to resort to only slow songs is not the norm, though, and should be done only when extreme measures are needed, or if you know for sure that the guests are much more into slow dancing. In most cases, people will dance to fast songs and are expecting them.

Special Songs for the Guests

My wife and I really wanted everyone to feel special at our wedding reception and to know we were thinking of them on our wedding day, so we had the DJ sprinkle in the First Dance songs of our married guests throughout the evening. We did not tell them we were going to do it. It was so cool to see their faces light up when they heard their special song. This was something that made the evening more memorable and romantic for everyone.

Requests

Couples are encouraged to give the DJ a "must play" music list and a "do not play" music list. This is very important — in fact, it is a must. You don't want the DJ to play a song that reminds you of an ex, the day your dog died, or a song that you just hate or are tired of. This is especially important with the group dances, such as the Macarena, the Chicken Dance, YMCA, etc. People love these songs and people hate them. Let the DJ know your preferences.

Most DJ's give their clients sample music lists and ask them to circle songs and cross off songs; as the final step, the bride and groom attach a separate document of music requests that they have compiled.

I occasionally get lists from clients that request enough music for five or six receptions! I usually laugh when I get them, and then let them know that it would be impossible to play them all (unless they wanted to schedule a thirty-hour reception). Keep in mind that most receptions last between four and six hours. The DJ will usually average between fifteen and twenty songs per hour, depending on the length of each song. Another point to remember: Some of the classic songs from the '50s and '60s tend to be much shorter than today's hits.

But it is not necessary (or even recommended) that you pick out every song. Give the DJ some leeway to read the crowd and make adjustments when necessary. If you give him a strict playlist and he plays a few of your song requests that nobody dances to, what will he do next?

Don't worry; if you hired a reputable, experienced DJ, he will not be choosing music for his own gratification. His one and only goal should be to make sure you and your guests have an amazing time, and he will play whatever it takes to make that happen.

Also, give him the space to play requests from your guests (which he will get). When they hear their request played, they feel more connected to the reception, and their energy level goes up. And that's what we want!

I have had other clients who give me no requests at all, except for the First Dance. They usually tell me something like, "We trust you, Rich. Just play some fun music and get people to dance!" While I have been able to do that countless times over the years, it's not the most ideal way to approach the music. What makes the reception special and fun for brides and grooms is to hear some of their favorite songs and artists. It makes it more personal.

Try to give the DJ at least a hint as to what you both like — a few of your favorite artists or songs — or at least let him know the genre of music you prefer. Or tell him what radio stations you listen to when you are in the car. Knowing what you like will help the DJ create a party that is more enjoyable for you.

Lighting for the Dancing

Some banquet facilities automatically dim the lights during an evening wedding reception when the dancing begins. This is something you need to be very careful with. Find out from the facility what they normally do. The truth is that some facilities turn the lights down too much, so that you can barely see the person you are with. Not only is that a safety hazard (especially for some of your older guests), but most people like to actually see the person they are with.

Dimming the lights too much also can affect the quality of your photos and video since the professionals who offer those services will now have to use bright flashes and lights, which can cast shadows on the walls and make some people look like ghosts.

There is the argument that some people feel less inhibited and relaxed when the lights are lower, so they would most likely dance more. In some cases, that may be true. On the other hand, I've had some amazing, high-energy weddings, with packed dance floors, that took place during the middle of the day with the sun shining into the room.

The bottom line: If you are going to dim the lights, dim them just a little. And when the lights are low, you can always add candles to the tables, which makes for a nice ambience.

Chapter Seven

Special Dances

Some of the most memorable moments of your wedding reception will come from your special dances. Here are some things to think about.

The First Dance

Every time my wife and I hear our First Dance song on the radio or play it on our computer, we get a little emotional. I'm getting misty-eyed just thinking about it right now! The First Dance is something very special and a moment you will remember forever. So choose it wisely.

Some people really look forward to this moment, while others cringe at the thought of a room full of people gawking at them as if they were animals in a zoo.

If you are both dancing machines, you have nothing to worry about. But if there are four left feet between the two of you, you may need to sway back and forth (slowly) to the song. Or you may want to look into dance lessons. Either way, you should practice your First Dance before the wedding day.

Why? Because you may find out that the tempo of the song is much faster or much slower than you thought, making it very hard to dance to. Practicing beforehand allows you to figure out how you are going to dance to that particular song.

Most slow songs are fine, and there is nothing to worry about. But you'd be surprised at how many times I've seen brides and grooms with worried looks on their faces after they realize that their chosen song wasn't very easy to dance to. Play it safe and listen to the song in your living room a few times to get a feel for the rhythm. To add a little fun, you may even want to plan certain moves, including perhaps a dip at the end.

A Choreographed First Dance

If you just don't feel comfortable on the dance floor, a choreographed First Dance may be the way to go. It's also a great idea if you want to wow your guests, especially if accomplished dancing is something they would have never expected from you.

You can do it! Just find a reputable dance studio nearby and inquire about private lessons for weddings. Some studios even offer a free sample lesson, so you can see if you will like their type of instruction. Then you can decide what genre you want and find a great song to match. Your guests will be floored, and you will have something to remember for years to come.

To create even more of a wow factor for your guests, do not tell anybody you are doing this — not even your parents! I've seen dozens of standing ovations over the years following a surprise choreographed First Dance.

An Important Note

If you decide to have a choreographed First Dance, make sure your DJ has the *exact* version of the song you want — the one you've practiced with. This is very important because some songs have many different versions, including a radio edit, an extended remix, an EP version, and an album version.

If you tell the DJ your First Dance song is "Unforgettable" by Nat King Cole, he will most likely just play the version of the song that he has in his library. But which version is it? The original? The remastered version from 2000? The remastered version from 2003? The duet with his daughter Natalie? Playing the wrong version of the song can result in your moves not matching up with the music.

I certainly don't want to scare you, and this is nothing to worry about if you take precautions. If you don't want to take any chances, give the DJ the artist name, song name, and album name, along with the exact length of the song. Or if you want to make it really easy, give him the CD or buy the correct MP3 version of the song for him on iTunes or Amazon.com and have it e-mailed directly to him.

Fading Out the First Dance

If you just don't like the idea of being out there on the dance floor all by yourselves, are not really into dancing, or don't know how to dance at all, some people suggest having the DJ fade out your First Dance song after a minute or two, instead of playing the entire song. I highly discourage this. First, people will notice. Second, if there are guests who really like that song and are singing along to it (or just enjoying it), they will be disappointed when the DJ fades it out.

The best thing to do is to have the DJ, after the first minute or two, invite the other guests to join you on the floor. Then all eyes will no longer be only on you.

The Fake First Dance

You've probably seen videos online of couples starting off their First Dance with a traditional slow song, then breaking into a completely different song that is wild and crazy and fun. Many of them have choreographed their moves too. This has been done a lot, and in many cases, people don't find this unique anymore, unless you come up with something absolutely different and fun.

Don't copy a video you've seen online. Anything you do should be different. You might be able to come up with the idea yourself, especially if you just want to do a parody of an online video, or you may want to enlist the help of a professional dance instructor. You can even incorporate the bridal party into the mix once the music changes to the second song. Done right, this can be something very fun and memorable for your guests.

Keep any fancy dance numbers a surprise, with the exception of the person who should be capturing it on video.

The Bridal Party Dance

This dance was popular in the '70s, '80s, and '90s, but not too many people do it these days. In fact, I completely removed it from my regular schedule years ago, and I do not recommend this dance to my clients. The bottom line, especially since this is supposed to be a slow song, is that most people would rather dance with their significant other rather than another member of the bridal party. (Of course, this dance would be okay if all the bridal party members were couples in real life, but that is rare.)

If you want to do a fun choreographed dance with the bridal party, that's another story. I do two or three weddings a year in which the bride and groom dance with the bridal party to "Thriller" by Michael Jackson. It's pretty funny to watch.

The Anniversary Dance (aka the Longest-Married Couple Dance)

The DJ invites the bride and groom and all the married couples onto the dance floor. One minute into the song, the DJ or MC says, "If you've been married for less than one day, please leave the dance floor." This is always a fun moment, because it catches the guests by surprise. Laughter and smiles fill the room.

Then the DJ begins to weed out other couples. Thirty seconds later, he says, "If you've been married for less than five years, please leave the dance floor." More couples will leave, and you'll get more laughs and "oohs" and "ahhs" from the guests watching. This continues until you have the longest-married couple on the dance floor.

It's important for you (and the DJ or MC) to make sure all the married couples are in the room before this starts. Also, the MC must know how long the longest-married couples have been together so he knows what increments to choose when eliminating them from the dance floor, and when to slow down as he approaches the longest-married couple.

Once the MC has the last couple alone on the dance floor, he can congratulate them and ask them their advice for achieving a long-lasting marriage. You'd be surprised at some of the emotional and sometimes very funny answers people give. This is a nice opportunity to present the longest-married couple with a gift — flowers or a bottle of wine — as a way of saying "Thank you for inspiring us."

This is always a crowd favorite, especially if you have grandparents, family members, or friends who have been married for forty or fifty years. The Anniversary Dance is highly recommended at all weddings unless, of course, you don't have many married couples in attendance.

The Honeymoon Dance (aka the Money Dance or the Dollar Dance)

In this dance, your guests pay to dance with you! In some cultures, this dance is expected and the bride and groom receive pressure from the parents or grandparents to do it, even though some couples would rather avoid it.

The Negative Side

Some guests find this dance in poor taste because you are asking the guests for money, even though they've already given you a gift. Only about 5 percent of my clients do this dance, and I usually don't recommend it because it eats up too much of the dancing time and drains the energy of the guests. But if you are low on funds or are spending all your money on the wedding, this is a good way to get a little rebate.

Just don't expect a ton of cash. You may get a few hundred dollars out of it. So you need to ask yourself: Is the time it will take out of your reception worth the payoff?

The Positive Side

The Honeymoon Dance is a great way for you to spend thirty seconds or so with each guest on the dance floor. If you don't really need the cash, you can have the DJ announce this as "The Charity Dance" and donate the money to your favorite charity. That would be a cool and positive twist.

Whether you want to do the Honeymoon Dance because you need the money or because it has been a long-standing family tradition, there are some things to keep in mind. The best thing to do is to make it fun and keep it moving along so people don't get bored; otherwise, it can easily eat up twenty to thirty minutes of your wedding reception. If you have a lot of things on the schedule, or if your priority is open dancing, it's best to skip this. If you still want to do it, here are some suggestions:

> * Have a bridal party member or family member monitor the lines of waiting dance partners to make sure they keep moving. Every thirty to forty seconds, this person should tell the next person in line to cut in.

> * Bring a bag of clothespins for the guests to use to attach the bills to the groom's suit. This can make for a fun picture after all is said and done. The bride can hold a pouch or small

purse for the guests to put her money into. Or you can have your line monitors hold small jars or decorative boxes for the money.

* Most people use slow or mid-tempo songs. You can also use upbeat songs if the thought of slow dancing with some of the guests creeps you out.

* If you want to make things a little more upbeat and light, you can make this dance a parody of sorts and play money-themed songs. Here are just a few:

"For the Love of Money" by the O'Jays

"Money Money" by Liza Minnelli

"Money for Nothing" by Dire Straits

"Rich Girl" by Hall & Oates

"How to Be a Millionaire" by ABC

"Money Talks" by AC/DC

"Can't Buy Me Love" by the Beatles

"Money (That's What I Want)" by the Flying Lizards

"Rich Girl" by Gwen Stefani

"If I Had $1,000,000" by Barenaked Ladies

"Money Money Money" by ABBA

"Gold Digger" by Kanye West

"Opportunities (Let's Make Lots of Money)" by the Pet Shop Boys

"She Works Hard for the Money" by Donna Summer

"Take the Money and Run" by the Steve Miller Band

"Mo Money Mo Problems" by Notorious B.I.G.

"Money" by Pink Floyd

Chapter Eight

The Cake-Cutting

This is always a favorite time for the guests since they know they will be eating dessert soon. It's also very unpredictable because they don't know if the bride and groom are going to smash the cake in each other's faces.

I personally don't like the idea of the face-smash, because it's not very romantic. It also ruins the bride's makeup and can cause delays while she cleans up. In some cases, if the bride has used a makeup artist, that person has to completely reapply the makeup.

But if you have always envisioned shoving frosting up the nose of your sweetie, I guess you are going to do it, no matter what I say.

Looking for something different that will get people to talk and raise the energy level in the room? Try one of these fun alternatives!

Cupcakes

If you want to do something fun and cool and different, try cupcakes at your reception, instead of the traditional wedding cake. There's something very magical and childlike about unwrapping a cupcake and eating it. Cupcakes also add personality to your reception. And anytime you are adding personality and uniqueness to your reception, you are adding positive energy!

One fun option is to create a tower of cupcakes to stand in for the traditional cake. This allows you to have two or three different flavors and can offer your guests a variety of choices. You can even have the baker make an extra-large cupcake to place on top of the tower, so you can still do a traditional cake-cutting.

Some of the very traditional guests at your wedding may not like the cupcake idea, but the majority of the people do — because cupcakes are fun!

Pies

I was very surprised at the guests' reaction the first time one of my clients had a pie table at their reception instead of the traditional wedding cake. The guests absolutely *loved* it! They hovered around the table, wondering when they were going to get to cut themselves a delicious slice. In fact, this is going to sound amazing, but every time I've had a client who has done pies, there was much more excitement than I've ever observed with a traditional cake.

There's something special about a sweet slice of apple, banana creme, key lime, or blueberry pie with a flaky crust that really gets people salivating. Some consider pie a comfort food, so maybe that has something to do with it. Whatever the reason, pies are always popular.

The last two times my clients had pie tables, a family member who was well-known for her baking skills baked them all as a gift to the bride and groom. Now that is an amazing (and tasty) gift.

Groom's Cake

This trend is more popular in the Midwest, but it's starting to gain popularity in other states. If the groom is a big-time sports fanatic, surprise him with a smaller groom cake adorned with the logo of his favorite team. If he is obsessed with motorcycles or something else, make that the theme of his cake.

Birthday Cake

I always think it's classy when my clients honor a guest whose birthday is the same day as the wedding, even though everyone is there to celebrate the wedding. It really shows that you don't have a big ego about the day being "all about you." Arrange for a small, ceremonial birthday cake and have everyone sing "Happy Birthday" to your friend or family member.

Cake-Cutting Music Suggestions

Here are some great songs that will add some fun to your cake-cutting!

"Sugar, Sugar" by the Archies

"How Sweet It Is (To Be Loved by You)" by James Taylor or Marvin Gaye

"Pour Some Sugar on Me" by Def Leppard

"Lucky" by Jason Mraz & Colbie Caillat

"Sweetest Thing" by U2

"L-O-V-E" by Nat King Cole

"Cut the Cake" by the Average White Band

"Recipe for Love" by Harry Connick Jr.

"That's Amore" by Dean Martin

"Hit Me with Your Best Shot" by Pat Benatar

"When I'm Sixty Four" by the Beatles

"Grow Old with You" by Adam Sandler (This is a short song, so choose another to follow it or you will need to cut the cake quickly)

"Ice Cream" by Sarah McLachlan

"Theme from Jaws" by John Williams

Chapter Nine

The Bouquet & Garter

The bouquet and garter tosses are traditions that have stood the test of centuries, but they appear to be slowly fading away. Only 50 percent of my clients do either of them. Still, with the right crowd, they can be a lot of fun.

By the way, if you choose not to do either of them, that is perfectly fine. Do not cave in to the pressure of a friend, a bridesmaid who happens to be single, or a family member. It's totally up to you.

If you'd planned to do the bouquet and garter toss after some open dancing, but the DJ has finally gotten everybody out on the floor and the place is really rockin', it's best not to stop the dancing just to do the bouquet and garter tosses. Don't worry about the timing of things at that point. It's better to keep the momentum going, when possible.

The Bouquet Toss

The bouquet toss is sometimes more like a full-contact sport. It's amazing how motivated some of these ladies are to get their hands on that thing. They take this pretty seriously!

It's funny to watch too. If you have a large number of single women in attendance, many of them will be expecting the bouquet toss. There are many ways you can do it, but I will focus on just a few of the most popular methods.

Over-the-Shoulder Toss

This is the most common bouquet toss, in which all the single women line up behind the bride on the dance floor. Many MC's will simply say, "On the count of three, ladies. Ready? Okay! One, two, three!" Then the bride tosses the bouquet over her shoulder. Some photographers will ask you to do a "fake toss" to make sure they get a great picture before you do the real one.

Before you make the toss, look behind to calculate the distance so you know how hard you have to throw it. Otherwise, it may shoot over everyone's heads and land on the floor, on someone's table, or on the cake. Or it may anti-climatically plop on the floor three feet behind you. Also be aware of chandeliers or low-hanging light fixtures. It's common for the bride to take a picture with the person who catches the bouquet.

The Exploding Bouquet (aka the Break-Away Bouquet)

This is a cool idea if you have more than a few women and you don't want anyone to feel left out. It also works if you have very few women, in which case you invite all the women (married or not) to the dance floor.

Simply toss out a bouquet that is actually five or six smaller bouquets held together only by your hand. After you throw it, the small bouquets break away and fly in different directions. You can even take it to the next level and tie a ribbon with a fortune or a charm to each bunch of poesies. The fortunes can be serious, funny, or sentimental, depending on your personality.

Bouquet Presentation

This is a great alternative to the traditional bouquet toss if you are not going to have many single women at your reception or if some of your female guests may find it embarrassing or demeaning. Just present the bouquet to someone celebrating an anniversary, someone who is recently engaged, someone who gave you a lot of support and guidance while you were growing up, or even your grandmother, if you are close to her.

Tell the MC why you want to present it to that particular person so he can share the story with your guests. Or if you are outgoing, you can grab the mic and tell everyone yourself!

Other Tips

If you want to avoid singling out your unmarried guests, or if you don't have many single women in attendance, have the DJ invite all the women (married or not) to the dance floor.

Music Suggestions for the Bouquet Toss

Here are a few fun songs for the bouquet toss. I usually get the ladies to dance for a minute before the bride tosses the bouquet.

"Single Ladies (Put a Ring on It)" by Beyoncé

"Dancing Queen" by Abba

"This One's for the Girls" by Martina McBride

"Girls Just Want to Have Fun" by Cyndi Lauper

"Ladies' Night" by Kool & the Gang

"Man! I Feel Like a Woman!" by Shania Twain

"Lady Marmalade" by Labelle

"Oh, Pretty Woman" by Roy Orbison

"All That She Wants" by Ace of Base

"Material Girl" by Madonna

"Girls, Girls, Girls" by Mötley Crüe

"American Woman" by Lenny Kravitz

"Hit Me with Your Best Shot" by Pat Benatar

"Wishin' and Hopin'" by Ani DiFranco (my personal favorite)

"P.Y.T." by Michael Jackson

"Brick House" by the Commodores

"I'm Every Woman" by Whitney Houston

"You Sexy Thing" by Hot Chocolate

"Chapel of Love" by the Dixie Cups

The Garter Toss

Now we come to the part of the reception that many guys are terrified of. Do they really think they have to get married if they catch it? It's pretty funny to see guys hiding in the back of the room, guys pretending they've dropped something on the floor, guys making a quick exit because all of a sudden they need to use the restroom or get something from their car, and others pretending they can't hear what's going on while being completely fascinated by a photo of the board of directors at that particular country club.

Of those who actually make it to the dance floor, some have their arms crossed or in their pockets and some stand way in the back or off to the side, while others are sipping on their beers with that look that some people get when they are getting ready to sit down in the dentist's chair. Poor things.

It doesn't have to be like this. The good news is that you can make the garter toss more fun for the guys. The options described below are also great alternatives for those who want to provide something more unique or who find the typical garter toss boring.

Garter Sports

Tying a particular sport to the garter toss is a surefire way to inject some energy into it — especially if the groom is a big-time sports fanatic.

After the groom has fetched the garter from his sweetie's leg, he can wrap it around a mini football or Nerf ball and toss it to the guys, who will fight till the death to get their hands on it. You can even kick it up a notch if the ball has the logo or autograph of a player from one of your favorite football teams.

Make sure the DJ plays a sports-themed song like "Monday Night Football" or something familiar from ESPN. You can even play your college fight song. Another option is to use the same song your favorite local sports team uses when the stadium or arena announcer introduces the players before the game.

If the groom is not into football, pick another sport. Do the toss with a mini soccer ball, baseball, or hockey puck. Make sure the tossed item is plastic or stuffed so nobody gets injured if they are accidentally hit in the head with it.

Non-Sport Toss

Don't have many sports fans in attendance? Well, what are they into? Do you have a bunch of nerds who are into sci-fi and *Star Wars*? Great! Toss a stuffed Obi-Wan Kenobi or R2-D2 doll or whatever you can think of that is fun. Just find a theme and then find a prize related to that theme.

Everything but the Kitchen Sink

This can be one of the most fun and silly things you can do at a wedding reception, and it always gets a lot of laughs. One of my clients did it just a couple of weeks ago, and it was so funny. The bride sits in a covered chair. The groom pretends he is reaching up her dress, but instead he is reaching underneath the chair cover to grab items that were placed there before they started.

What things, you ask? Granny panties, a mousetrap, a whip, handcuffs, a rubber chicken, a checkbook . . . you get the idea. Use these or come up with your own! It's a lot of fun, and you'll have the guests laughing and taking pictures. Of course, the last item to be pulled out should be the garter.

Music Suggestions for the Garter Toss

Here are some suggestions for music during the garter removal and toss.

"Let's Get It On" by Marvin Gaye

"Cherry Pie" by Warrant

"Pour Some Sugar on Me" by Def Leppard

"Legs" by ZZ Top

"Another One Bites the Dust" by Queen

"Foxy Lady" by Jimi Hendrix

"Theme from *Mission: Impossible*"

"Oh Yeah" by Yello

"Danger Zone" by Kenny Loggins

"U Can't Touch This" by MC Hammer

"You Can Leave Your Hat On" by Joe Cocker

"Keep Your Hands to Yourself" by the Georgia Satellites

"A Little Less Conversation" by Elvis Presley

"Wild Thing" by Tone L?c

"You Sexy Thing" by Hot Chocolate

Chapter Ten

Games & Other Interactive Fun

Some guests can be very conservative. Even though they are sweet, positive people who are truly enjoying the experience of your celebration, it would still take a crowbar to pry them out of their seats to dance. And that's okay. We do not want to force them to do anything they don't want to do.

If you are expecting a conservative group, you will definitely need your DJ or MC to be more interactive in order to get them pumped up. Fortunately, even the conservative groups who are not big on dancing do like to laugh. Playing some fun or silly games will get the giggles flowing. I've even had some clients with very outgoing guests who still wanted to do games, just because they love them.

Here are a few games that can be a lot of fun and can entertain those who are glued to their chairs.

Deep Down in Your Sole (aka the Shoe Game)

The bride and groom sit in chairs on the dance floor, back-to-back. The bride should have a high-heeled shoe in her hand and the groom should hold an athletic shoe. (Make sure someone remembers to bring these extra shoes to the reception so they don't have to use the ones they are wearing.) Barbie and

Ken dolls can be used instead of the shoes, or different-colored ping-pong paddles.

The MC will ask the bride and groom a series of questions to show the guests how well they know each other. "Who" questions work best. For example: *Who will be the decision maker as you start your new life together?*

The bride and groom are not allowed to speak, and since they are sitting back-to-back, they won't be able to see each other's responses. After each question, the bride and/or groom answer by raising their shoe above their head. Of course, in most cases the bride and groom raise their shoes at the same time, resulting in some hilarious moments. Here are some sample questions:

Who said "I love you" first?

Who mentioned marriage first?

Who makes all the decisions?

Who is the messiest?

Who spends more money?

Who is the best kisser?

Who is grumpier in the morning?

Who does most of the cooking?

Who is the better driver?

Who cleans more?

Who made the first move?

Who is more anal?

Who is a bed hog?

Who is always running late?

Who is the biggest baby when they get sick?

Who holds their alcohol better?

Who has the best taste in decorating?

Who has the best taste in music?

Who is the first to say "I'm sorry"?

Who was the first person to "pass gas" out loud in front of the other?

Who spends more time in front of the mirror?

Who's more likely to run a red light?

Who snores the loudest?

Who is always right? (this should be the last question)

Roman Hands & Russian Fingers

For this fun game, the bride needs to be blindfolded. The best man hides three paper clips on the groom's body in hard-to-find places, such as the back of his head, on his belt, or on his shoelaces. At the start of the game, have the best man hold up the paper clips so the guests can see them and have the DJ or MC announce that he is going to hide them.

The blindfolded bride then has to find all three paper clips on the groom's body, while the guests let her know (by shouting and cheering) if she's getting warmer or colder. In order to keep this game PG13, the paper clips should not go under clothing or in pockets, even though some brides may still go there. They should be somewhat visible.

Once the bride finds all three paper clips, the guests cheer and the game is over. Have the MC announce the action, play-by-play style, for more fun.

Which One Is the Bride?

This time, the groom is blindfolded. Five female volunteers sit in chairs on the dance floor. The sixth chair is occupied by the bride. The groom is expected to guess who the bride is by feeling the right hand of each of the seated individuals.

The MC should be on the dance floor, guiding the groom from one person to the next. He must tell the person to present her right hand to the groom (some left hands may have wedding rings and would be a tip-off). If the person has rings on the right hand, have her remove them for the game. Just before the groom begins his examination of the hands, replace one of the women with a man with a big hairy hand. You can also replace one of the women with a child who has a very tiny hand.

To kick this one up a notch, have the groom feel the women's feet or calves instead of their hands. If you do this, make sure you include a guy with *really* hairy legs. It's so funny to watch.

Which One Is the Groom?

Blindfold the bride, and this time have five male volunteers sit in chairs. The bride needs to guess which one is the groom by feeling the face of each guy. If the groom is clean-shaven, make sure you include a guy who has a mustache, goatee, or beard for some great laughs. You can even put a boy in one of the chairs. To make it even funnier, you can have the bride also run her hands through the hair of each guy.

Kiss Me Now!

The guests love to see the bride and groom kiss. Clinking water and wine glasses is a common way to get them to pucker up. *Note:* If you have kids at the reception, they may become obsessed with this idea and clink every couple of minutes. If you are okay with that, so be it. And if you'd like something a little more unique or fun, try one of the following options.

Putt for a Kiss

This is a great idea for couples who are big-time sports fans or just want to do something more fun. It works especially well if you are having your reception at a country club, but you can do it anywhere, really. You can probably find practice putting greens at your local sporting goods store. There are also many available on Amazon.com for between $10 and $50.

During the dinner, set up a putting green in the middle of the dance floor. The bride and groom will kiss only when a guest gets a hole-in-one. Have the DJ or MC make an announcement at the beginning of the dinner saying that clinking glasses is not allowed. Only a putted hole-in-one will result in a kiss. It's a pretty straightforward game and can be a lot of fun for the guests.

Sing, Sing a Song

This one creates a lot of energy and can be really enjoyable. It is done not individually, but by table. If the guests want you to kiss, the entire table has to stand up and sing a verse or a couple of lines from a popular song with the word "love" in the title or lyrics. Make sure the DJ is paying attention during the dinner because if he sees a table standing up to sing, he needs to fade out the background music temporarily, until they have finished singing.

This Is How We Do It!

In this game, your guests have to show you how to kiss! Provide the DJ with a list of names of some fun couples in attendance — the more fun and wild, the better. The DJ will call out the couple's names during the dinner and ask them to show the bride and groom how to kiss since they are newbies. After they are done, the bride and groom have to imitate how the couple kissed. This can get a little crazy, depending on how wild your friends are, but it can be great entertainment for your guests — and a lot of fun for you!

Pay per Kiss

During the meal, set up a heart-shaped jar on a small table in the middle of the dance floor, close to the head table. Guests are encouraged to put money in the jar if they want to see you kiss. The money will be donated to the charity of your choosing. Lots of kisses for a great cause! Make sure the MC announces the charity before the game starts.

The Centerpiece Giveaway

Most couples give their centerpieces away toward the end of the reception. If the flowers are in elaborate or expensive vases that belong to the florist, the MC should simply announce that the guests are free to take the flowers, but please leave the vases or they will be apprehended by security and taken to jail.

A simple announcement, such as "Harry and Sally wanted me to mention that you can take home the flowers that are on the tables," is pretty boring. Here are a couple of options to make the centerpiece giveaway more fun.

Closest Birthday

The most common way to give away the centerpiece is to give it to the person at each table with the birthday closest to the wedding date. If there is a tie (very rare), you can have the two narrow it down to the hour they were born.

Pass the Dollar

This is definitely my favorite way to give away the centerpiece. It's a fun game that creates great energy, and it has a surprise at the end that always gets some good laughs.

Have the MC announce that you are going to play a little game to give away the centerpieces. Then he says he needs one volunteer from each table to offer a dollar bill to use in the game. That person holds up the dollar bill when he or she has it ready. After each table has a dollar bill ready, the DJ starts an upbeat, fun song and the dollar bill is passed around the table. When the DJ stops the music, the person with the dollar bill thinks they've won the centerpiece, but they actually win the dollar bill. It's the person who was generous enough to offer the dollar bill who wins the centerpiece. This game is always a winner.

Video/Slideshow

Videos and slideshows can be a lot of fun, especially when cute (and sometimes dorky) child photos are included. The ideal length for a video or slideshow is eight to ten minutes. If it goes any longer, you risk boring your guests and losing some of the energy (even if the pictures are super-cute).

I recommend showing it at one of two times: toward the end of dinner or while the guests are eating the cake. I prefer to show it while people are enjoying the cake since there is usually a lull in the dancing at that point.

Another option is to run it on a loop during the cocktail hour, but that can get old after a while. If the video or slide show has music, make sure your DJ has a cable that can connect the 1/8-inch headphone plug of your laptop with his system, so everyone can hear it. If you want the DJ to play the music, instead of playing it directly from your laptop, make sure he knows what versions of the songs you want and give him the following info: the name of the photo segment, the name of song to be played, and how much of that song you want played. Here's an example:

> Tanya's Childhood Photos — Play song "Girls Just Want to Have Fun" by Cyndi Lauper (fade song at 2:45)

> Steve's Childhood Photos — Play song "Let's Hear it for the Boy" by Deniece Williams (entire song)

> Tanya and Steve's Dating Photos — Play song "You Make My Dreams" by Hall & Oates (entire song)

Chapter Eleven

The Last Dance

You have many options for ending your reception in a memorable way. Most people pick a romantic song and enjoy one last moment on the dance floor, surrounded by their family and friends, who dance with them. Others prefer an upbeat song to end the reception on a high note and keep everyone buzzing right into the parking lot and all the way home.

Avoid Fizzling Out

Some couples wait too long to play their Last Dance because they scheduled it at a certain time and they think they need to stick to that schedule. Then, at some point before that time, the guests slowly start to trickle out one after another until you only have maybe 20 or 30 percent of the people left.

This will sometimes happen at Sunday night receptions; the guests start thinking about the fact that they have to get up early the next day to go to work. It is also common at receptions that include lots of kids since most parents want to put them to bed at a certain hour.

Just because the facility gives you the place until a certain hour doesn't mean you have to use all of that time. In most cases, if you notice the guests are starting to leave, it's better to end the reception early and end with a bang!

Music Suggestions for the Last Dance

Here are some great songs that will add some fun to the end of your evening.

"Hit the Road Jack" by Buster Poindexter

"Closing Time" by Semisonic

"Good Riddance (Time of Your Life)" by Green Day

"Last Dance" by Donna Summer

"(I've Had) the Time of My Life" by Bill Medley and Jennifer Warnes

"Bye Bye Bye" by 'N Sync

"Happy Trails" by Van Halen or Roy Rogers and Dale Evans

"We Gotta Get Out of This Place" by The Animals

"Don't Leave Me This Way" by Thelma Houston

"New York, New York" by Frank Sinatra

"Friends in Low Places" by Garth Brooks

Chapter Twelve

The Big Send-Off

There are many ways to say good-bye to your guests at the end of the reception. Some people like to organize a big send-off instead of saying good-bye on the dance floor.

I once had clients who had a helicopter waiting outside the facility. I asked everyone to join them outside, and the guests stood there in awe as the bride and groom jumped into the helicopter with their suitcases and went straight to the airport to start their honeymoon. It was pretty amazing to watch them disappear into the sunset. Obviously, chartering a helicopter is a little extreme, but it worked well for them and made the end of the event very memorable.

On a more realistic note, here are the three most popular ideas for the send-off, if you want to add something special.

The Sparkler Send-Off

This one is very unique and can give you some great pictures, but be aware that in some areas using sparklers is illegal and/or a fire hazard. You will also need an assistant or two to hand out the sparklers and help the guests light them as leave the building. You should also have a couple of buckets of water or sand nearby, just in case.

Once the guests have formed two lines facing each other and all the sparklers are lit, someone will signal the bride and groom to come outside and walk through the people as they cheer and wave the sparklers in the air.

Make sure the photographer and videographer are close by to capture the scene as you walk through the two lines of guests. It will be a pretty cool video to play back at a later date.

The Human Tunnel

As with the Sparkler Send-Off, the guests form two lines facing each other. This can be done either inside the ballroom, from the dance floor to the exit doors, or outside, leading the way to your limousine.

Once you are ready to go, the guests will be asked to hold their arms over the space between them, forming a human tunnel. On the DJ or MC's cue, you race through the tunnel as the guests scream and cheer. This also makes for a great photo, so make sure your photographer and videographer are on alert. They can follow you through the tunnel, walk backward in front of you as you travel through it, or wait for you on the other end.

Party Poppers

Although more commonly used on New Year's Eve, party poppers can be a lot of fun at any time of the year. The DJ or MC gets everyone organized in two facing lines and someone hands out the party poppers — one for each person.

Once everyone is in position, the bride and groom walk between the two lines as the guests set off the poppers. Make sure the photographer captures this because it can be a pretty cool photo with confetti flying over the heads of the happy couple. Even better would be video that also records all the popping.

Bubbles

Instead of party poppers, some couples use bubbles. This option involves a few downsides, though. The soap in the bubbles can stain some fabric. And it's usually not a good idea to do this one on the dance floor or a tile floor because the soap from the burst bubbles can make the floor slippery and create a hazard. It's much better to do it on carpet or on the cement outside as the bride and groom head to the limo.

Chapter Thirteen

The Top 25 Wedding Regrets

After all is said and done, it's common for couples to think back on their wedding day and analyze all the little details. It's not surprising that some would have done a few things (or many things) differently if they had it to do over again.

Here is my list of the top 25 wedding regrets. These regrets come from brides all across the United States. You can learn *so much* from this list! Okay, I feel like Ryan Seacrest here . . . let's count them down to number one!

25. Interviewing potential vendors before you had the date and venue booked.

The date and the venue are the first two things you should secure, before working on anything else. Without those, wedding vendors can't let you know if they are even available and give you an accurate quote. Imagine interviewing three photographers and then finding out later, once you've picked your date, that none of them are available. What a waste of time. Plus, if you had your heart set on one photographer in particular, you're bound to be disappointed when you find out you can't have him or her.

Many vendors charge a different price for a Saturday versus a Sunday or a Friday, or they may charge a premium for holiday weekends.

Besides the date, I personally like to know the location as well because the time it takes to set up and access issues can vary greatly between one place and another, so that I may have to allow an extra hour or more for setup and an extra hour for breakdown. Some places charge for parking, which I also need to take into consideration when giving a quote.

In short, it's almost impossible for you to get accurate quotes when all the necessary information is not available. Here is a conversation I had on the phone with a bride.

> **Bride:** Hi, Rich. I just wanted to call and get a little information about your services and pricing.
>
> **Me:** Of course. I'd be happy to share some info with you. Let me first get the date of your wedding so I can make sure I am available.
>
> **Bride:** Well, we don't have a date yet.
>
> **Me:** Oh. Okay. What dates are you considering?
>
> **Bride:** Well, we are not sure of that either. We are thinking maybe in the summertime, maybe July or August. Although, we'd be open to a Christmas wedding because I heard some

venues offer great discounts on winter dates. Not sure yet.

Me: Do you know what day of the week?

Bride: We were going to do a Saturday, like most weddings, but may consider a Friday or a Sunday, if our favorite place is not available.

Me: So you've looked at some venues? Cool. Which ones are you considering?

Bride: Well, actually, we just saw a couple of venues online, but haven't seen any in person yet. We're not sure, really. Who knows? We may end up doing it in my parents' backyard!

When I get these calls, it's pretty frustrating, as they are a waste of time for both of us. Why spend thirty minutes on the phone with someone or swap ten e-mails with them if you don't even know if they will be available on your date?

The savvy bride-to-be tries to avoid stress. Wedding planning can be very time-consuming, and if you get the cart before the horse, before you know it you've spent thirty hours researching vendors when you don't even know if they will be available once you've chosen your date.

Yes, I get it; you are excited to plan your wedding, and it may be fun for you to check out websites of vendors and imagine how your wedding day will unfold.

You can choose your wedding dress without a date. And the style of your invitations. Even your colors. But not your wedding vendors.

Do yourself a favor — first pick your date and book your venue. Then start reaching out to potential vendors to get more information. That will help keep your stress and frustration levels to a minimum and make the best of your precious time.

24. Not changing into more comfortable shoes or sandals once the dancing started.

It's common to see the bride and bridesmaids halfway through the reception sitting in their chairs with their shoes off, massaging their feet with a look of pain and discomfort on their faces.

One easy solution is to bring a second pair of shoes or sandals to change into once the dancing starts. I've even had clients offer sandals to all the female guests. In such cases, I make the announcement right before the start of the dancing and point to a box of sandals on my table. There is always a mad dash toward me to get them. And they all disappear! Obviously, it's not necessary to provide them for everyone. Most women just kick off their shoes at some point and dance barefoot. (If that's the case, have the MC announce that no drinks are allowed on the dance floor — broken glass and bare feet are not a good mix.)

23. Not getting all the pictures you wanted.

Many couples just want the day documented in candid shots and don't want a lot of formal pictures. For others, those formal shots may be a big deal because your wedding day may be sort of a family reunion, with relatives coming in from all over the country or even from other countries.

If that's the case, make a list of all the pictures you want to have taken before, during, and after the ceremony and during the reception. Give a copy to your photographer and emphasize how important this is to you. You may want to give another copy of the list to the wedding coordinator or a friend of the family, and that person can help corral everyone for the photos, which will save you time so you can maintain the schedule you have in mind.

Avoid having the MC make announcements every three minutes that certain groups of people need to leave to have pictures taken; this can make your venue feel like a train station or an airport, where there are frequent public announcements, rather than a setting for an elegant private affair.

The taking of photographs is one of the main reasons receptions go off schedule. Photographs are vital in preserving the memory of this special day, but the photo sessions need to be well planned so they don't delay things and reduce the time you'll have available for dancing.

22. Printing programs for the ceremony.

Many people feel presenting a formal printed program for the wedding ceremony is very elegant, but what typically happens after the ceremony? About 50 percent of the programs are left on the chairs. And probably another 25 percent end up being left in the banquet room at the end of the reception. With a few exceptions, the guests who do take them home soon consign them to the recycle bin. Obviously this is not one of those regrets that will sit in your gut for a lifetime. But if you hate to waste paper and want to save some trees, skip the printed program for the ceremony.

Besides, most people follow along in a program just to see how much time is left before they get to eat and drink. You will have their attention more fully and they will be more present if you don't give them a program.

21. Not having alcohol available at the reception.

You and your family may not drink, but that does not mean you should not have alcohol available for your guests. You don't need a full open bar that offers every drink under the sun. But you do need alcohol if you want a high-energy reception.

Why? Because people feel less inhibited when they drink. It loosens them up. And when they are loose, they dance more. Plus, some people don't get out as much as they used to (because of babies or children or hectic lives), so many are actually looking forward to having a few drinks.

Some religions don't allow alcohol consumption at wedding receptions, so if that's the case for you, there's not much you can do.

If budget is a concern, keep it simple: beer and wine. That's all you need to make everyone happy.

Have I DJ'ed wedding receptions without alcohol, but the guests still danced and had a great time? Of course. But such occasions are very rare. At a reception without alcohol, the MC has to be very interactive, and you also need to have an outgoing group of people. And on some such occasions, I have occasionally seen guests head to the parking lot during the reception to drink from a flask or bottle they kept in their car, after which they pop a breath mint or two and come back inside.

The easiest solution is to make sure you have booze for those who enjoy it. You can enjoy sparkling cider if you don't drink.

20. Not making the wedding "Facebook-free."

It's become more common for the bride and groom to ask me to announce that they want the wedding to be Facebook-free. In other words, please do not take pictures and post them to your Facebook wall.

Why would the bride or groom care? It's more like why would they not care! Imagine all the people you connect with via Facebook whom you *did not* invite to your wedding. How do you think they will feel when they see photos of the celebration and everyone having a good time? Plus, you may have coworkers as Facebook friends whom you did not invite. Maybe you don't want them to see certain things. This is definitely something to consider. You also don't know what some people might post after a couple of drinks. It's better to not risk it.

19. Planning a huge wedding and spending thousands of dollars for the sake of the parents.

If you really don't want to have a big wedding with a ton of people, don't do it. Just because your parents say it's "the right thing to do" does not mean you have to do it. What do you really want to do, deep down in your heart?

Do you want a small, intimate wedding or one to which you invite just fifty people? *Do it!* Do you want a destination wedding in Hawaii? *Do it!* Especially if your future spouse feels the same way, *do it!* Do you want to go to the courthouse and get married on the steps outside, then celebrate at In-N-Out Burger? *Do it!* A drive-thru Elvis chapel in Vegas? *Do it!*

One of my best friends had her wedding in Hawaii, and she knew that not everyone was going to make it. She even knew that some people might complain. But she did it anyway. Only fifteen or so people made it, but it was a great time. And she never regretted it.

Most people will want to make sure that their immediate family and very best friends can make it. Then they share pictures with the rest or maybe have a barbecue or invite them for some other more casual gathering.

Don't cave in to outside pressure and invite people you really don't want to be there. Do what you want to do, and do it for the reasons that make sense to you. Some people skip the big wedding because they would rather spend those thousands of dollars on buying their first home.

My wife and I easily could have had a guest list of 250 people. But we had 75. Why? Because we wanted something more intimate, with only our closest friends. And we wanted to buy a house. We don't regret it at all. It's okay if you want to have a huge wedding. Just don't do it to please someone else.

18. Choosing a larger venue that had multiple events going on.

Imagine showing up to the venue where you are going to have the biggest day of your life and running into two other brides with their bridal parties taking pictures. That's not going to make you feel all that special, but it's the chance you take when you book a place that has multiple banquet rooms.

Also, in such venues sometimes the sound will travel though the walls from the party next door so you may hear the *thump, thump, thump* of the music in the next room just as your father is making a sentimental toast before dinner. Does this happen? You bet. I've even seen guests from one wedding putting gifts for the bride and groom on the gift table of a completely different couple. I had to grab an employee of the hotel to monitor the gift tables and make sure the gifts were going to the right couple.

17. Not smiling when you walk down the aisle.

I am really surprised at how many times I have seen the bride walk down the aisle without a smile. My guess is that she is very nervous. Most likely most brides don't even know they are doing it. But they will get a *big* surprise when they get their pictures and video back.

Remember to smile when you walk down the aisle. If you have to, repeat to yourself as you are walking, "Smile, smile, smile." And tell your bridal party members to smile too as they walk down the aisle and as they stand next to you at the altar. Some people look so serious. It's not a funeral!

16. Going on a crash diet to fit into a wedding dress.

Be careful about extreme dieting before the wedding. Over the years I've seen a few brides faint during the ceremony. I later found out they had been starving themselves so they could fit into the wedding dress and look good for the pictures. No, no, no. Be realistic. And be yourself.

15. Not hiring a wedding planner or a "day of" wedding coordinator.

If you get stressed easily, tend to worry about everything, or are not very organized, do yourself a favor and hire a wedding planner to assist in selecting vendors and venues, planning the design and decor, and creating and managing the schedule of events.

At least hire a "day of" coordinator to manage your wedding day and to make sure all your plans are carried out. It will be the best money you've ever spent.

Don't assign the job to your maid of honor or someone in your bridal party. They don't have the experience to handle such a task and will probably only get in the way or annoy your vendors. Plus, they should be celebrating with you and not working.

14. Not opting to pay the overtime facility fee to extend the reception another hour.

My wife and I made this mistake and we regret it. Picture yourself having the time of your life at your wedding reception. The music is great, the energy level is high, and you are dancing up a storm with the guests. Maybe you have finally gotten free from the photographer and have just started dancing too and are loving it. Then you notice the reception is going to end in five or ten minutes. What do you do? Should you just let it end?

During a few of my receptions each year, I see the bride and groom huddled in the corner ten minutes before the scheduled last song. They may even look over at me a couple of times during the discussion. I know what they're talking about. They are discussing if they want to extend the reception for another hour. Sure, they may have to pay the facility and the DJ more to extend it. Is it worth it? Based on this topic being one of the top 25 regrets, the answer is obviously *yes*.

Brides have written to me after they returned from their honeymoons, telling me they had the time of their lives but should've extended the reception by an hour. Of course, you want the reception to end on a high note. But if you didn't get much dancing in, or just feel like dancing more, do yourself a favor and extend it an hour.

If you don't even want to have to think about something like this at your reception, try to negotiate a longer contract with the facility and DJ *before* the wedding day. This problem is more common when people plan three- or four-hour receptions.

13. Sharing too much information about the wedding with friends and family *before* the wedding day.

Of course, you should think of your guests when you plan your wedding day; you want them to enjoy it. But you don't need to tell them everything you plan to do. It's okay to keep even family members in the dark. Surprise them on your wedding day!

Many years ago I MC'd a wedding for a bride whose father was a Harley Davidson fanatic, and everybody at the wedding knew it. She asked me if there was anything we could do at the wedding to honor him in some way . . . something cool or funny. I came up with the idea of playing the sound effect of a revving Harley motorcycle engine as he escorted her down the aisle during the wedding ceremony. She loved the idea, so I tracked down an MP3 of the sound effect. He had no idea we were going to do it, and neither did the guests. And guess what? Everyone loved it! The guests could not stop laughing and smiling. They talked about it during the cocktails. They talked about it during the dinner. Heck, they are probably still talking about it now.

This fun idea would have gotten a completely different response if everyone had expected it to happen.

Another important consideration: People will be very quick to give their opinion about your wedding day and what you are planning, so it's probably better to not tell them. They don't need to know everything. And the more you tell them ahead of time, the less exciting it will be for them on the wedding day itself.

12. Having a very large bridal party.

A few years back I did a wedding that had fifteen bridesmaids and fifteen groomsmen. Including the parents and grandparents, I had to introduce forty people at that wedding! The funny part was, they had only eighty guests total, so the room was half empty when we did the Grand Entrance since half of the people were lined up behind me for the introduction.

Keep in mind that you have to manage all those people before the wedding, coordinate dresses and tuxes, and so much more. You are even supposed to buy a "thank you" gift for everyone in the bridal party. That's a lot of gifts!

My wife and I could've chosen more people to be in our bridal party, but I ended up having just a best man and my wife had two maids of honor. That was it. And it was perfect for us.

Just because a person had you in their bridal party does not mean they have to be in yours. Just because that person is your brother or sister or cousin does not mean they have to be in your bridal party. Trust me, it's much better to keep it smaller and simple.

11. Not spending more money on the photographer.

Not everybody knows how to shoot weddings. Just because your cousin has a good camera does not make her a wedding photographer.

Some couples choose a friend to shoot their wedding. Sometimes it works out, but many times it doesn't. Just because your friend has posted some incredible sunset photos or amazing photos of his garden on Facebook or always volunteers to take pictures at company events or parties doesn't mean he knows how to shoot a wedding.

Some amateur photographers don't even have a backup camera, so if their equipment goes on the fritz, you have no images to remember your day.

There are so many things that need to be captured and so many things to know about wedding photography. In most cases, it's just not worth it not to use a pro.

Make sure you really love the portfolio of the photographer you are considering. Then meet with that person to get a feel for his or her personality.

And make sure you love that personality, because you are going to be spending more time with the photographer than with any other vendor.

10. Using a friend as your wedding planner.

Just because she is organized or just because she volunteered for the job doesn't mean you should make a friend your wedding planner. Having someone you know help out with little things is okay. Having your friend marching about with a clipboard and ordering people around is completely different. I've seen this many times, and usually amateur wedding planners just get in the way of the professional vendors, who already know what they need to do.

9. Budgeting for your wedding using recommendations from a website or magazine.

Most budget calculators or suggestions offered online or in magazines are so off target, it's not even funny. In fact, it's really sad. How can they tell a bride she needs to spend a certain percentage on one thing and a certain percentage on another? That's like the diamond industry, which created a campaign that said you should spend two months' salary on an engagement ring. In my opinion, it's the most ridiculous thing ever. But many people follow such advice!

Some wedding websites tell a bride that she should spend 50 percent of her budget on food, 10 percent on the photographer, 10 percent on the DJ, etc. That's crazy. Everyone is different, and people have different priorities and goals. Some put more value on the location versus the food or more on the DJ versus the flowers. Some brides want to have a $10,000 dress and then serve food from El Pollo Loco.

What's worse is that some websites give an average price for a particular wedding vendor, but what they don't realize is that different regions and cities in the country vary in price tremendously. By contacting three to five vendors in each category and getting quotes, you will be able to determine the average price in your area for that vendor. Then you can more wisely factor in price as you decide who you want.

8. Not booking a photographer for the entire day.

I can't tell you how many times a photographer has come up to me during a wedding and said, "Hey, just to let you know, the bride only hired me until nine o'clock, so you need to do the cake-cutting, bouquet, and garter in the next ten minutes. Otherwise she'll have to pay me for overtime to capture those photos or she won't get them."

The problem is, it may not be the right time to do the cake-cutting. Maybe the dancing just got ramped up and everybody is having the time of their lives on the dance floor. And now I'm being asked to stop the dancing, even though it just started, just so the photographer can snap those photos before he leaves? Talk about a surefire way to kill the energy in the room. To avoid that scenario and get all the pictures you want, make sure you hire the photographer for the entire day.

7. Worrying about everything and not being able to relax.

If you are stressed, most likely your fiancé will be stressed. When people are stressed, it's difficult for them to live in the moment and enjoy the experience. Stress is what causes people to drink too much at their receptions — always a bad idea.

When your guests pick up on this stress, their moods will be affected as well. People feed off your energy at the reception. If they see you smiling and laughing and bouncing around the room, they will most likely do the same. If you appear tense or unhappy or worried, it's hard for others to have a good time. They will notice.

Soon your wedding day will be over, and you will wonder where the time went. Yes, the time will fly by . . . guaranteed. People miss out on the fun at their weddings all the time — all because they are stressed. Don't make this mistake yourself. Live in the moment and enjoy every second. You'll be glad you did.

6. Using a friend to be the DJ.

Just because your friend has 6,000 songs in his music library and some speakers does not make him a DJ. And even if he gets paid to DJ in nightclubs, it's not the same thing as doing weddings. He most likely won't have a clue about the program and how to make it flow and about being an MC.

And how will he respond when certain unexpected things happen at the reception?

Plus he may play only rap or house music. You may think that's okay if you are a big fan of rap or house, but I have a feeling your parents, grandparents, and some other guests are not going to like a whole afternoon or evening of that music.

5. Not using the microphone to thank everyone for coming.

Tell the MC you want to take a few moments to thank everyone for coming. It just takes a moment and your guests will love it. This is typically done at the beginning or the end of dinner or after you cut the cake. The guests really respond positively to hearing you on the microphone.

And don't forget to thank your parents. If they have been generous enough to pay for your wedding day or you are very close to them, you need to acknowledge them on the microphone and thank them. Some parents will be very hurt if you don't.

Even if they didn't pay for the wedding, thank them for their support and for everything they've done for you in your life. It's touching. It's special. Add it to the program so you don't forget.

By the way, if you are absolutely terrified of the microphone or are shy, put your thoughts down on paper. Write a few sentences about what it means to have everyone there to celebrate with you. Acknowledge the guests who traveled long distances. Then have the MC or the best man or a family member read your message to everyone.

4. Not using a microphone and speakers at the ceremony.

It's so frustrating to go to a wedding and not be able to hear the bride and groom exchange their vows. It's such a special, romantic moment, and it's sad that a lot of the guests miss it.

If you are going to have a small ceremony, with between thirty and sixty people in attendance, it may not be necessary — if you have an officiant who articulates well. Just make sure that both of you speak distinctly too. For larger ceremonies and for ceremonies in areas with lots of background noise, using a microphone is a must.

Not being able to hear the vows as they are exchanged is one of the biggest problems with weddings on the beach. The sound of the waves drowns out the voices of the bride and groom and the officiant. A battery-powered public address system is an option, but be careful of the lavaliere or lapel microphones that some DJ's put on the groom and the officiant. If it's a windy day, they will pick up every sound and will annoy the guests. In some cases, it's much better to have a cordless microphone on a stand in front of the officiant.

3. Letting the pictures and video dominate the day.

This happens all the time, and it is sad. The bride and groom are so worried about getting pictures of every person and in every situation that they cannot enjoy the reception. Some photographers pull the bride and groom off the dance floor or interrupt them just as their dinner is being served to continue working on the long list of photos they've said they need. They disappear from the reception for thirty to forty minutes, only to return to a cold plate of food. And you know what usually happens at the end? I hear something like these sad comments from the newlyweds at the end of the reception:

Darn, I didn't even get a chance to dance at my own reception.

I only danced three songs. Where did the time go?

Thanks for playing all our favorite songs, Rich. I heard them and wanted so badly to dance, but we had to take all those pictures and talk with everybody.

Sure, you will have all those pictures. But you will also remember not being able to dance and have fun at your own reception. You'll look at those pictures once a year; you'll see a photo of people dancing at your reception and having fun and you'll think, *we should be in that picture!*

Do yourself a favor and hire a photographer with a relaxed approach. Posing everybody in a particular, pre-established way is the ultimate time suck. It can be very stressful to watch the time tick away at your reception while you're off posing for photos.

2. Not spending enough money on the DJ.

Do you *really* like the DJ you are considering? Or did he just give you one of the lowest price quotes? To ask ten DJ's for price quotes and then just go with the lowest price is taking a huge risk. Are you absolutely confident that he is going to offer you outstanding customer service? Does he have a great personality? Does he have plenty of experience, and can you find great reviews of him online? Have you seen video of him at his past receptions? Did you meet him in person, and did you connect with him immediately?

Don't settle for a mediocre DJ just so you can save a few hundred dollars. It's not worth it. Your entire reception is on the line (not to mention the memories you will have forever), and you will most likely regret it, as so many other brides have.

Drum roll, please! The number one regret is:

1. Not hiring a videographer.

This is far and away the top regret of brides. The excuse they almost always give is that they didn't have enough money in their budget. But then some of these same brides planned a four-course meal for everyone that even included an intermezzo and an open bar with top-shelf alcohol. You need to establish your priorities. I've been to weddings where they served absolutely incredible two-course meals that everyone raved about. Think about switching your meal from a four-course to a two-course affair. Or maybe you can spend a little less on the flowers or offer just beer and wine for the guests instead of a full open bar.

People who have hired a videographer are always happy that they've captured those special memories forever so they can relive them again and again. My brother plans a special dinner with his wife every year on their anniversary and they watch their wedding video. How romantic! If you really want a videographer, find a way to make it happen.

Chapter Fourteen

Final Thoughts

Unexpected things can happen on your wedding day. They usually do. In most cases, when you hire the right professionals, you and the guests will never know they even happened. The way you react to the things you do know about will be a big indication of how your wedding day will turn out. It's that simple.

Having the right attitude makes all the difference in the world on your wedding day. You can freak out about the rain, the centerpieces that had seventeen roses even though you paid for eighteen, or about the kid who pulled the bride-and-groom cake topper off the cake and ate it.

Or you can just blow off such things (even laugh them off) as insignificant in comparison to the big picture. Try to keep your sense of humor on your wedding day. Things may go wrong, but does that change your love? No way!

It was such a pleasure to share this advice with you. I'm confident that if you use many of these ideas, your reception will have lots of energy and you and your guests will have a huge amount of fun.

A last word: Don't assume your DJ will know and/or implement these ideas. You need to be proactive and tell him what you'd like. Have fun!

Acknowledgments

To Silvi
Thank you for your love and support. I love you.

To my Mom
Thank you for making me possible.

To Jeffrey Messerschmidt

Colette Barnes

Vince Ramirez

Jessie and Sara Garcia

Lucie and Sam Silveira
Thank you so much for your help.

To Dave and Katie Orsburn
Thanks for being wonderful clients and for letting me use your cool photo on the cover.

About the Author

Rich Amooi is a writer, radio personality, and award-winning DJ. He is happily married and lives in San Jose, California, with his amazing wife and their very hairy dog.

Rich also writes romantic comedies. Find out more about his next novel at richamooi.com

If you feel this book has helped you in any way, please leave a review online wherever you bought it. Thanks so much!

Made in the USA
Columbia, SC
05 September 2018